P9-AGL-456

LIKE BROTHERS

MARK DUPLASS

LIKE BROTHERS

BALLANTINE BOOKS | NEW YORK

JAY DUPLASS

WITHDRAWN

Copyright © 2018 by Freebie LLC and Jippet Inc.
Foreword copyright © 2018 by Mindy Kaling

All rights reserved.

Published in the United States by Ballantine Books, an imprint of
Random House, a division of Penguin Random House LLC, New York.

BALLANTINE and the HOUSE colophon are registered trademarks of
Penguin Random House LLC.

LIBRARY OF CONGRESS CATALOGING-IN-PUBLICATION DATA
Names: Duplass, Mark author. | Duplass, Jay author.
Title: Like brothers / Mark Duplass and Jay Duplass.
Description: First edition. | New York : Ballantine Books, [2018]
Identifiers: LCCN 2017057278 | ISBN 9781101967713 (hardcover) |
ISBN 9781101967720 (ebook)
Subjects: LCSH: Duplass, Mark | Duplass, Jay. | Actors—United States—
Biography. | Motion picture producers and directors—United
States—Biography. | Screenwriters—United States—Biography. |
BISAC: BIOGRAPHY & AUTOBIOGRAPHY / Entertainment &
Performing Arts. | HUMOR / Form / Essays. | BIOGRAPHY &
AUTOBIOGRAPHY / Personal Memoirs.
Classification: LCC PN1998.2 .D75 2018 |
DDC 791.4302/8092 [B]—dc23
LC record available at https://lccn.loc.gov/2017057278

Author photographs on pages 296–97: © Carissa Dorson.
Duplass Brothers logo on page 299 by Mark Duplass and Jay Duplass.
Images on pages v and 292 are from the personal collection of
Mark Duplass and Jay Duplass.

Printed in the United States of America on acid-free paper

randomhousebooks.com

2 4 6 8 9 7 5 3 1

FIRST EDITION

Book design by Simon M. Sullivan

I love you, but less so when
you're punching me in the face.

Definitely Start HERE

WHETHER YOU'VE BEEN waiting months for this book to come out, or you are at an airport wondering who these two extremely regular-looking guys are on the cover and why some idiot let them write a book . . . either way . . . Hi. Nice to meet you, kind of. We are genuinely excited for you to read our book.

We've tried to offer a collection that is entertaining, funny, and (ideally) a bit useful. Something that you'll remember once you're done with us. This book is filled with essays on all kinds of things. Some are specific to our film and television careers, some to our twentieth-century childhood and our twenty-first-century parenting experiences, and some relate to random pop culture that made an impression on us along the way. Most, however, are our attempts to make you laugh, cry, or emit that quiet "mmmm" sound under your breath when you've been gently enlightened. Essentially, we hope that when you finish this thing you will turn to us with glee (like our mom did) and exclaim, "There's something here for everyone!"

Needless to say, we'd like you to read the essays in *Like Brothers* from front to back, in the order we chose. But it's also cool if you want to pick and choose stuff. Let's say you're an aspiring filmmaker or artist trying to figure out how two brothers from nowhere special with no special connections managed to build something from nothing. If that's you, you could read the Roman-numeral chapters and skip the rest. You'd miss a lot, but you'd get the history of our journey and a bunch of our secret widgets as to how we carved a career inside this insane Hollywood system without anyone else's help. Or, if that's not you, you could skip the Roman numerals and read the rest of the book: essays on the wonderful/terrible nature of collaboration as well as a bunch of other random things that fell out of our brains.

Either way is fine. We just humbly ask that you read it. It will teach you some things. Because that's what books do.

Your friends,
Mark and Jay

FOREWORD
MINDY KALING

Do NOT PUT Mark and Jay Duplass on your sitcom. Ever. I made that mistake. Six years ago, they guest-starred on my show, *The Mindy Project*. They were just supposed to come in, play funny midwife brothers, and leave. But within a day and and a half, the entire cast and crew liked them better than me. There was something about Mark and Jay's Southern affability, their genuine interest in the people around them, their low-key stylish clothes, and their fascinating Hollywood stories that drew everyone to them. They even sang and played the guitar really well. How eyeroll-emoji-inducing is that? Suddenly everyone on my show had abandoned me to be around Mark and Jay and hear stories of how they'd made their wonderful films *The Puffy Chair, Safety Not Guaranteed, Cyrus, Tangerine*, and many more. Then everyone wanted to know what it was like to star in their own television shows, *Transparent* and *Togetherness*. It was all too much for a leading actress to hear, so now they are banned from set.

But somehow I still like to hang out with them. Just privately. Because they're funny, they're woke as hell, and they have a way of making you feel like the best version of yourself. They're artists, with that kind of tireless entrepreneurial spirit that inspires. When you hear them talking about their projects, suddenly *you're* excited about making a movie too! Maybe *you'll* direct a film that you wrote! Maybe *you'll* go to Sundance and have Ted Sarandos from Netflix throw obscene money at you for all your artistic endeavors! These two act, they write, they foster talent, they take chances on young artists, and they do it all while being married and raising kids. I guess white men *can* have it all. And I'm glad this book exists to explain how. And to make you feel like I feel when I'm hanging out with them.

In closing, I'd just like to say this:

Wright. Ringling. Jonas. I'm sure you could name a bunch of famous brother teams. They're all garbage compared to Mark and Jay. I can't wait for you to read this book. But please don't mention them if you ever run into me.

Love,

Mindy

Los Angeles, California

CONTENTS

PROLOGUE

THE ROYAL *WE* is a tricky thing. It's certainly helpful at times. It allows us to share that collective first-person-plural voice that makes us The Boys (a label that's stuck since childhood). The royal *we* perfectly sets up those inspiring twenty-to-thirty-word quotes in articles written about the beauty of our long-term film and TV collaboration. How we share the same brain. How one pronoun can encompass us both. Basically, we use it to talk about ourselves because it brings our voices together. Making us stronger.

But it also sucks sometimes. Because there's a distinct lack of *I* in that *we*. And the bizarre, undefinable edges that make us uniquely ourselves get rubbed out so that the *we* can come across more clearly. Is it reductive? Sometimes a little bit. Sometimes a lot. But it's for the greater good, right? Because no one wants to listen to Lindsey Buckingham's solo record (sorry, Mr. Buckingham, as much as we love your technically proficient acoustic finger-picking, this is just a reality). People want to listen to Fleetwood Mac. That magical blend of disparate talents that creates the special soup you can eat all week, not just on Tuesday afternoon when you're hungover and feeling weird.

So we use the royal *we*. And in the past ten years or so, The

Boys have become a brand of sorts. The ideal creative duo. And we feel many people's hopes and dreams pinned upon us. That we will stay together and live in collaborative bliss forever. That others might build a similar bond with one of their siblings or, even better, have kids who get along like we do. So, people pleasers that we are, we play into this fantasy with idyllic sound bites about our collaborative process:

"Two heads are better than one."

"It's hard making good art, and we'd rather put aside our differences and get each other's help."

"Whatever personal issues we have are quickly dwarfed by our love for each other and our understanding that we need each other to navigate this world."

And all of this is true, but not entirely so. What's also true is how oddly difficult it is to do what we do and keep this thing moving forward. How we struggled for years trying to make a decent piece of art together. How we finally broke through, with each other's help, and created a new model of making films and TV in the process. How this success has brought its own set of challenges. How our intense closeness through the years has caused trouble for our girlfriends and now our wives. How we stand next to each other in this life, trying desperately to hold on to each other and keep The Boys together, while at the same time lovingly pummeling each other in the face so we can get a breath of air that doesn't already smell like the other one's breath.

And how on a daily basis we cry more than grown men should. But laugh a shit-ton as well.

LIKE BROTHERS

I.

It is dark.

It is late.

It is 1984.

We are lying next to each other in one of our twin beds. But, predictably, we are not asleep. We are talking about life. And our dreams. And the great mystery of cable television.

"Jay?"

"Yes, Mark?"

(Silence. Mark has always loved the dramatic silence. I am older by four years and should find this annoying, but I love this about him.)

"When is it coming?"

"Soon."

"How soon?"

(I take a moment to mitigate expectations and not get my seven-year-old baby brother too excited.)

"Dad said by next week it'll be here."
"What does it look like?"

(*I actually do not know, but I have a few theories.*)

"I'm not sure."
"Is it, like . . . a big cable?"
"I think so?"
"Do they just drag it down the street and plug it into the house?"
"I don't think that's how it works."
"How does it work?"
"I don't know."

(*Mark thinks on this. Wide-eyed. Young mind grappling with what it all means.*)

"What is going to happen to us, Jay?"
"Nothing crazy. I don't think. Or maybe everything."
"I'm so excited."
"Yeah, me too."

(*Pause.*)

"Jay?"
"Yes, Mark."
"I have something to confess."
"What?"

(*Again, the dramatic pause.*)

"I don't know what cable is."

*(I try extremely hard not to laugh. I am careful never to con-
descend, because he is smart and very sensitive. Still, I am
an older brother and can't help myself. . . .)*

"If you don't know what it is, then why are you so excited
about it?"

"I don't know. I just . . . I heard you talking about it to your
friends. And . . . I can tell how excited you are about it. So . . .
I got excited about it."

*(Not an extremely eloquent response, but quite prophetic in
many ways as to the nature of our unique brotherly bond
and complex relationship to come.)*

"It's going to be bringing a lot of movies, and TV shows,
and a bunch of new channels into the neighborhood."

"Do you think it's gonna change everything?"

"I don't know."

(Pause.)

"Jay?"

"Yes, Mark."

"When we grow up do you want to get houses next to each
other?"

"Definitely."

(Mark considers this.)

"Do you think . . . we could share the same cable? Or do we
have to get different cables for each house?"

"I could probably figure out how to share one."

(Mark believes me. He believes that I am very good at this kind of thing. Good at everything, actually, if you asked Mark in 1984. This was a huge part of building my confidence.)

"What happens if we wanna watch different movies but we share the same cable?"

"I think we'd have to watch the same movie."

"So what do we do if we ever want to watch a different movie at the same time?"

(We both consider this question. It's a troublesome thought. Might there come a time when our interests, and therefore our lives, diverge? The question hangs over us like a fat black cloud for a moment. But then we smile. Because this is a ridiculous thought. We will always want to watch the same movie. We will always live right next to each other. We will always lie in bed at night and talk about our lives and our dreams.)

Two weeks later, cable arrives at our home.

And everything changes.

THE WOOG

Do YOU FEEL weird inside? We do. All the time. Sometimes we call it depression. Sometimes we call it anxiety. Sometimes we just call it "The Woog." As in "I'm feelin' Woogie today." At the core of this weird feeling is a sense that there are, at minimum, two people inside of us at war. And we don't know how to make them get along.

"I'm gonna stay up all night and write and put on my weird hat and two different socks and smoke weed and eat cereal and maybe pizza too and try to crack a new kind of story and make something fascinating and different and I don't care if I never make any money because I'm an artist who is trying to represent the underrepresented and create empathy for all. . . ."

And.

"I probably should go back to business school. And learn how to buy and sell companies and make millions and millions and maybe billions and use that money to start charities. This is the better way to live. For others. Not for myself and for my artistic vision. That's . . . that's kind of a load of selfish horseshit in the end. . . ."

And then some other voices start to pop up. And it's hard to tell if they are subsets of these two main people or if they are actually secondary characters that also live inside of us.

"I just want to live a quiet, simple life with my family. I want to stay home and be there at all times with my kids. Read to them. Cook for and with them. Play board games. Just be a good parent and husband and, in the end, just kinda *be* . . .

"TEACHERS! That's what the world needs now. Leadership for young kids who don't have positive role models. Give myself and everything I can to them. An innocent child needs a thoughtful role model, and even though I'm not perfect, I am likely willing to give more than what I hear the average burned-out public high school teacher can give, so I should get my teacher's license and . . .

"The world is hard enough. Who am I to think I can help and *save* anyone? I'm just an average-intelligence person trying to get by. It's enough just to make my own way in the world. I should just go inside myself. Stop talking and start listening. Get small and find a small sliver of happiness in the world and hang on to it for dear . . ."

You get the picture.

Do you ever feel this way? Hopefully not. And if you don't, feel free to skip to the next chapter.

But if you do . . . we want to say sorry. Sorry you feel conflicted like we do. That you are uncertain as to what the right path is in life. Sorry that you want so badly to be useful but also happy. To be inspired but also at peace. To make change but also just get by.

But we also want to say . . . CONGRATULATIONS! Because, in our opinion, you may just be part of a dying breed. There will be fewer and fewer of you, and because of that and so much more, you are truly special.

Here's our theory:

When our parents got married, it was a time when people mostly married young. And in many cases, they married without fully vetting whether they would be a good matrimonial fit. Let's face it, they often got married because their religion said "no sex before marriage" and they really just wanted to start humping and not go to hell for it. They got married because they were sexually attracted to each other. And that attraction was often a result of the "opposites attract" theory. So when we were made, we were made from very different individuals who came together mostly because they liked the way the other smelled, as opposed to any long-lasting traits that made for a sustainable partnership. Hence, the two different people inside of us.

This new generation is different. They are taking longer and longer to find their mate. They are more thoughtful about finding the right partner, and they often don't get married until age forty or later and have kids soon after. Because of this, they are truly dialing in the perfect mate for themselves. As a result, the people who join up in this generation tend to have many core elements aligned, such as hobbies, interests, family-work values, and personality type. And when this generation has kids, those kids will be a product of the somewhat homogenized personality aspects of their parents. Thus they will be more "of a piece" and suffer less of the frenetic, multiple-personality-esque weird Wooginess that we suffer.

As much as it is a somewhat painful existence to live with the Woog hovering over us, we also kind of love it. We feel that the combination of our goofy, creative, fun-loving mother and our incredibly efficient, intelligent, ass-kicking, type-A attorney father has made us . . . unique. Our silly, creative engine burns through our mom, and our ability to make it a practical, sustainable business for us and our friends comes directly from our dad.

There was a great bumper sticker in Austin when we lived there that celebrated a zip code of unique Austinites from a specific time and place. It said "78704, Keep Austin Weird." We take comfort in that bumper sticker when the Woogieman comes to get us. We don't fight him as much. In fact, we try to let him in now, and celebrate the emotional kaleidoscope in which we live.

II.

WITHIN SIX MONTHS of cable's arrival in 1984, we were hooked. But not in the way our peers were hooked. We lived in a suburb of New Orleans called Metairie, which offered cheap land and wide streets for families with young kids. On weekends, most of those kids rode their bikes, bought candy from the Time Saver across the street, and talked about *Star Wars*. And while we did some of that, we were more taken by some of the other programming that HBO had to offer. What many people don't remember about the early days of HBO is that the programming wasn't exactly curated for the time of day it was airing. So we'd wake up on Saturday, start with a viewing of *Kramer vs. Kramer*. Then we'd roll right into *Gandhi*, or *Ordinary People*. And then lighten the mood with *The Deer Hunter* or *Sophie's Choice* before finishing the afternoon off with *Coming Home*. Every now and then we'd take in *Fletch* or *Every Which Way but Loose*, but mostly we were watching the hard-hitting dramas of the seventies and eighties. And we loved them. But not in a pretentious "We're more erudite than *Star Wars*" kinda way. We just loved watching people emote, and feel, and we deeply connected with the spirits of those dealing with divorce, hunger, PTSD, and death. It wasn't that we were morbid either, we were just . . . into it.

Around the same time, our dad brought home our first video camera. This was huge. Not metaphorically. Literally. The thing was a beast. And, like most dads in the eighties, he was terrible with electronics and couldn't figure out how to use it, so he basically left it in our hands. Jay, being the older-smarter-stronger one, picked up the manual and became the first one to figure it all out. (Side note: To this day, I do not know how to read an owner's manual or assemble anything, because Jay was always there to do it.) But Jay needed a second person to carry the separate VTR tape deck (which attached to the camera via an enormous cable) and ideally act in the "films" he was brewing. I got the job. And thus began the two-person filmmaking team known as the Duplass Brothers, circa 1985 (ages twelve and eight).

Now, let's be clear. There are tales of the childhood films of the Coen Brothers and Spielberg showing the seeds of the great filmmakers they would eventually become. Our films were not like those. Ours were dull, boring, uninspired, and fairly stupid. We re-created *The Blob* by throwing our beanbag down the stairs. We took a stab at remaking *The Invisible Man* by taking quick shots of an empty pair of shoes walking around our living room. We randomly filmed our ears for a while. Yeah.

Eventually, however, we cracked our first narrative: the story of a young karate master whose home was invaded by a burglar. The film itself is lost to us forever, but we remember the story perfectly, so we've taken the liberty of re-creating the script here. For posterity. And because it still makes us laugh.

INT. MODEST HOME—DAY

A KARATE MASTER, played by an eight-year-old Mark Duplass, casually saunters around his living room, thinking about stuff. He takes in his surroundings and accomplishments with an air of self-satisfaction. He also wears his KARATE GI, though he appears to be doing no karate at the moment. [NOTE: *The Karate Kid* had just come out and we were taking karate lessons. We had a rented gi. We felt we had to use it.]

Suddenly, the Karate Master HEARS A NOISE. He sees something offscreen that scares him and causes him to flee to another room, but we don't get to see what he sees. [NOTE: We were not aware that we should have shot and shown what he actually saw.]

Then, finally, we see the BURGLAR, played by our neighbor Brandt, who didn't really want to be doing this. The Burglar slooooooooooooooooowly turns the door handle and walks into the living room. The cameraman (Jay) follows him in, filming him from the side as he looks around the living room. He pulls out a "cigarette" (blue Bic pen) and "lights" it (mimed).

Suddenly, the Karate Master appears in the kitchen, just beyond the Burglar and his cigarette. He sees the Burglar and *runs toward him*. He jumps into the air, *kicking the cigarette out of the Burglar's hand!* [NOTE: We shot this about seven times, each time moving the cigarette farther and farther from Brandt's face so I wouldn't injure him with my poorly aimed kick. The resulting shot pictured Brandt holding the cigarette about five feet from his face before I kicked it loose. It was unfortunately a bit leading as to what would eventually happen, but we did get the shot.]

There is a quick scuffle (very quick, too quick) and the Burglar throws the Karate Master out of the house.

CUT TO:

Sometime later. Much later. So much later that the Burglar now seems to have taken ownership of the house at this point? Sure. In fact, he is so comfortable that he seems to be casually lifting weights on the floor of the living room. [NOTE: These were three-pound pink hand weights that came with our mother's Jane Fonda workout video set.]

In an impeccably composed wide shot, the Karate Master comes *flying into* the living room, not unlike Cato in the Pink Panther films, and *jumps* on top of the Burglar. [NOTE: We did this shot in one take. I accidentally dropped my knee into Brandt's crotch. The pain he experienced and the yelp he emitted were, according to Jay, "like gold." We kept it in the original film. Just one of those happy accidents. Happy for Jay, at least. Not for Brandt.]

CUT TO:

More time has passed. [NOTE: These transitions of the early Duplass Brothers cinema are quite jarring. Probably a "choice." Now we are in . . .]

INT. MODEST HOME—DINING ROOM—DAY

The Karate Master has assumed control of his home once more. He is setting up dinner for himself (bowl of cornflakes) but he is unaware that a mysterious presence lurks just beyond him. [NOTE: Even though the

Burglar is directly in my sight, Jay tells me to pretend
that I don't see him. A brief argument ensues about the
plausibility of this scenario. Jay tells me that it'll be
fine, but I can't bear to perform the untrue nature of
Jay's direction. Then Brandt tells us he's leaving in five
minutes to go to JCPenney with his mom. So I cave and
we simply get on with it.]

When the Karate Master finally "sees" the Burglar,
he notices that this time the Burglar is holding a *knife*.
A knife that already has blood (ketchup) on it, though
he hasn't killed the Karate Master yet? Sure. Not quite
sensical, but it was super dramatic, so we went with it.

As the Burglar closes in on our clearly doomed
Karate Master, the Burglar utters these final, chilling
words:

BURGLAR: These days, you cannot . . . trust . . . *anyone*.

CUT TO BLACK
THE END

We watched the film over and over that day. Three scenes.
Five minutes. All working together to fulfill a dramatic climax. We were so proud of ourselves. We showed it to our parents, who did what proved to be the perfect thing. They
neither praised nor dismissed it. They simply observed,
gently supported the effort, and quickly left us to figure out
the next steps.

That night, we slept together in one of our twin beds, as we
always did at that age.

"Mark?"

"Yeah?"

"When you brought in the bowl of cornflakes for the dining room scene, why did you pick the spot by the window?"

(*I consider Jay's question.*)

"I don't know. It just felt like where I should do it. Why?"

"I was curious because that's exactly where I imagined you should go, but I forgot to tell you to go there before we started filming. But you still kinda knew to go there."

"Uh-huh."

(*I am only eight and not quite getting it yet.*)

"Do you ever feel like . . . like we share the same brain sometimes?"

"Totally. Like we're the Corsican Brothers or something?"

"Exactly! I miss that movie. Why don't they show that anymore?"

"I don't know."

"It's like they keep showing *Ordinary People* and they can only show one movie about brothers."

(*I grow quiet for a moment. It may be time for us to finally drift off to sleep.*)

"Jay . . . I don't think I want to watch *Ordinary People* anymore."

"Why not?"

"It . . . the brother part. It makes me really sad."

"I understand. It makes me sad too."

(Jay, always the fantastic older brother, picks up the mood for us.)

"Maybe we can make a movie about brothers next weekend."

"That would be cool."

"I love you."

"I love you too."

We both say good night at the same time and fall off to sleep. And we know exactly what you're thinking right now. That the whole situation we just described is a load of bullshit. No eight-year-old and twelve-year-old brothers sleep in the same twin bed. And even if they did, they certainly wouldn't speak to each other so lovingly.

But we did.

TOP 10 FILMS OF ALL TIME *

We were once asked to come up with a list of our all-time Top 10 films. Then we laughed that person out of the room. Because it's difficult enough for one filmmaker to come up with a list of Top 10 films, but to ask for a consolidated list that represents both of our favorites . . . that's just cruel. But we thought about this potential undertaking on and off through the years, and we felt we may have been ducking an interesting challenge. So we decided to take a crack at it by listing our individual favorites and then, not unlike a jury, trying to compile one overall list that satisfied us both. It began like this (and took way longer than we imagined):

MARK'S TOP 10 FILMS	JAY'S TOP 10 FILMS
American Movie	Rocky
Raising Arizona	American Movie
Starman	Margaret
Same Time, Next Year	Raising Arizona
Tootsie	Henry Fool
Rocky	The Horse Boy
Hoop Dreams	You Can Count on Me
The Crying Game	The Black Stallion
Dumb and Dumber	Dumb and Dumber
The Cruise	Close-Up

* *To be continued . . .*

MOVIES NOT MEETINGS

THERE'S AN INTERESTING ritual in the film industry called the "general meeting." Not sure if other industries have this, or a version of it, but it fascinates us to this day. A general meeting usually comes about because one of the parties is a fan of (or trying to get something from) the other party. For instance, if we loved someone's short film and wanted to meet them to discuss possibly working together, we would ask them for "a general." Likewise, if a studio or producer was a fan of our work, they might ask us for the same. Sweet and harmless. But not really.

In our first year in Los Angeles, we took about a hundred general meetings. Possibly more. And a rhythm started to develop. We would drive across town to their offices. Wait for a bit. Then we'd all sit together and do some general ass-kissing and getting to know each other. And, at the end of the meeting, we would inevitably all say something to the effect of "We should definitely find something to do together."

As you might imagine, very rarely did we actually find something to do together. In fact, I think it's safe to say that not one of our general meetings has directly resulted in doing anything more than driving home and wondering if we wasted a couple of hours. Maybe *wasted* is a strong word, but we are filmmakers and we have to work extremely hard and long hours to get our stuff made, so at the very least we began to question whether we should be putting our time into something more fruitful.

And as we questioned this age-old ritual of the general meeting, something more disturbing occurred to us: People in this town (and possibly in this industry altogether) spend about ninety-nine percent of their time talking about the potential of making something. And a large chunk of that time is spent in a general meeting that will most likely never amount to anything. And no one seemed to be talking about this problem. Wasn't this an obvious waste of time that was easily identifiable? From our perspective, yes. So we made a decision: Maybe we should cut down on the general meetings.

When we proposed this concept to our representatives, they were shocked. Won't people be offended if we don't take the general meetings they ask of us? Even if not, how would we make those long-term connections that would ultimately lead to success in the industry? The feeling we got, overall, was one of "This is just not done." We were on speakerphone during this call with our reps, looking at each other in amazement. It was as if we were trying to extract ourselves from some sort of cult that might bludgeon us to death if we tried to leave the compound. So we did what we normally do in these situations. We took a walk.

MARK: I feel like they're gonna be mad at us if we don't take the generals.

JAY: Totally. But . . . I don't know. My deep gut says this is wrong. That this whole process is just . . .

MARK: Bloated and inefficient and false?

JAY: Yeah. I mean, how many hours do you think we've spent, travel included, doing these meetings?

(A little math. It starts to dawn on us.)

JAY: Two hundred? Maybe more?
MARK: Yep. And how long does it take us to write a solid draft
of a script?

(Quiet. A realization. Then, a sadder kind of quiet.)

Yep. It hit us like a heavy sack of diarrhea (sorry, gross, but
it really got to us). In all the time we had spent ass-kissing
and talking bullshit in those general meetings, we could have
written another script and basically eradicated the need for
those meetings.

After the initial shock and embarrassment, however, we
became emboldened.

We walked back to Jay's house, called our representatives,
and led with our chins. We told them we had decided we
wanted to *make* films, not talk about them. We even came up
with a clever and overly dramatic moniker for our newly
birthed philosophy: We wanted to "make movies, not meetings." We laid it all out there and let them know, in no uncertain terms, that we would not be taking general meetings. We
didn't want to be difficult, but we had our own way of doing
things and we needed to do what our gut told us was right.
Much to our surprise, our representatives were very understanding and respectful on the phone. They were clear on our
stance and validated everything we had to say. It was a small
victory but an important one.

A few weeks later, our main representatives ended up leaving that agency to go to an even bigger one. We were not invited to come along with them.

AIRPORT

#1

As our careers started to take off, we found ourselves spending more and more time traveling. We'd fly around the world to attend film festivals or to promote a new project. And we started to lament how much time it was taking away from our actual filmmaking and writing. What we didn't realize until later is that many of the seeds of our film stories were being birthed in our travel downtime. Particularly at airports, which are fantastic for people-watching. Not only are people generally at their worst while traveling, but they are forced to sit very still and quiet with each other, so their body language becomes incredibly demonstrative of their relationship dynamics.

We found ourselves becoming more and more obsessed with these odd pairings of people at airports. So much so that we began to build fictional stories about them. Some turned into entire movies that we made, some were used for interesting side characters, and some were just for our own personal amusement. When we signed on to write this book, we decided to record a few of these conversations and transcribe them. Here is one. Admittedly, a little bit edited so we don't sound like totally uneducated dipshits.

(Sitting across from us is a somewhat dowdy woman in her late fifties. Her posture emits low energy, maybe even sickness. She sits next to an extremely good-looking if not altogether intelligent-looking fellow who seems to be in his late thirties. They share a meal.)

JAY: Whoa.

MARK: Yep.

JAY: First thought is that she had him when she was, like, fourteen.

MARK: And for a while he didn't know who his real mom was.

JAY: Yeah, like, they lived with her mom and dad, and those two told him that they were his parents and she was his sister.

MARK: Cuz it was a fairly religious small town in Alabama where having kids out of wedlock that young just ain't cool.

JAY: They planned on telling him the truth after he graduated from high school.

MARK: Right. Get him off to college or wherever, but tell him right before he goes so he can process it outside of the house and get through his anger while he's establishing his independence.

(Giggling.)

JAY: They figured it would take him a year or so to get over it, but he'd be in a progressive environment, expanding his mind like most eighteen-year-olds do, and would ultimately understand and forgive them the lie. "I'm a college freshman and grown-up now. I understand how the world works and can sympathize!"

MARK: Good plan.

JAY: Great plan. Very emotionally evolved.

MARK: Didn't work out that way, though.

(Pause. We are trying to think where the story should go next. Neither wants to speak first and fuck up an idea the other may be having that could be great. It's quite a long silence. We are smiling.)

MARK: Because her parents died unexpectedly?

JAY: Oh. Shit. That's . . . that's kinda rough.

MARK: It would give her the chance to hold the secret that she was his real mother forever if she wanted.

JAY: True. But dark.

MARK: Other option is he accidentally found out when he was fifteen.

JAY: That's what I was thinking. He was looking for his old Gobots in the attic. Found a birth certificate.

MARK: Freaked the fuck out.

JAY: Ran away from home without saying anything to anyone—

(Suddenly the man leans over and kisses the woman on the mouth. Not just a peck. An openmouthed kiss.)

MARK: Okay.

JAY: Didn't see that coming.

(Giggling.)

MARK: Okay! Changing gears!

(Full on gigglefest.)

MARK: So . . .

JAY: So.

MARK: They are not mother and son. They are lovers.

JAY: For sure.

MARK: They met when he was, like, nineteen.

JAY: She was . . . thirty?

MARK: He was working as a waiter at her favorite lunch place. And they developed a friendly rapport.

JAY: Because she was hot.

MARK: And successful. She ran her own business.

(*Pause. Thinking.*)

JAY: One of those printing companies that were popping up everywhere in the early aughts.

MARK: A thousand business cards for $99?

JAY: Exactly. Started in a small warehouse outside of town.

MARK: Perfect. And she would bring clients to this lunch place because it was central between her warehouse and downtown.

JAY: And she always tipped him well because no matter how busy he was, he took care of her and treated her like she was big-time.

MARK: Exactly. Like he intrinsically knew she was trying to impress a client, so he served her as if she were the proverbial shit 'round these parts. And it helped her nail down her clients. But all of this was unspoken.

JAY: So she started tipping him even more.

MARK: And one day she asked him why he was working in a place like this. He was charming, good-looking, clearly better than this.

JAY: He had some issues with his parents. Dropped out of high school. This was his first job. They paid him decently. So he stuck with it.

MARK: She asked him to come see her offices when he got off work. Maybe she could find him a better job.

JAY: So he did. And she got him an entry-level job in her printing business.

MARK: And it was becoming clear to everyone else at work that, like, there was clearly a physical attraction between these two.

JAY: He had a missing mom figure. Filling in that gap.

MARK: She was busy and successful and maybe preferred a young stud to something more stable.

JAY: Before long, they began an affair. And the sex was incredible.

MARK: That whole "both of them being in their sexual prime" thing that people talk about.

JAY: And despite her initially viewing him as more of a boy toy, when her father passed he was emotionally great to her.

MARK: And she fell in love.

JAY: And so did he.

MARK: So they got married when he was just twenty-one. He didn't even invite his parents.

JAY: And things went well for a while. They co-ran the company, and he even started doing commercials and modeling for their printing business.

MARK: Yes! And he was awesome at it!

JAY: But then the shit hit the fan.

(*Pause. Thinking.*)

MARK: I got it. Because printing as a business started to crash with the advent of online advertising and the green movement. And the smaller start-ups were the first to go under.

JAY: And she worked her ass off to save her business. Not sleeping. Living very unhealthy.

MARK: And he encouraged her to just let it go. He had enough experience as a model and commercial actor that he could support them now on his salary if he branched out.

JAY: So she let the business go, and he became a very successful catalogue model for their area.

MARK: But it was hard on them and their marriage. Because being a model means that you are surrounded by young, hot models all day long.

JAY: And she was in her early forties now, but looked a lot older from the stress of her business being run into the ground.

MARK: He, on the other hand, looked better than ever. For whatever reason. Genetic lottery. But now that twelve-year age gap looked more like . . . a lot more than that. People even mistook them for mother and son.

JAY: And she became insecure about him being around young female models all the time. And she started drinking more. And just generally tanking.

MARK: And he promised his devotion to her. Reminding her that she was the one who saved him and made him who he is today. And that he would never leave her.

JAY: And she quickly replied that she didn't want him to stay with her because of what she'd done in the past but because he loved her for who she was right now.

MARK: And she looked at him sadly, and he looked into her eyes and said, "Of course I am with you because of who you are now."

JAY: Which they both knew was a lie.

MARK: Ugh. This is getting hard.

(We look at each other. Feeling deeply for this woman. Hoping that our story isn't anywhere near true. And also wanting them to win now.)

MARK: But it all changed last month.

JAY: It did?

MARK: Yeah. Something amazing happened. His birth mother, whom he'd never met, saw his picture in a JCPenney catalogue and reached out to him.

JAY: Right! He got really nervous. So his woman, who has been with him all this time, came with him to meet his birth mom.

MARK: And it went horribly. This guy's birth mother was a vapid, terrible person who only wanted to meet him so she could get connected in the modeling business herself.

JAY: It crushed him, and that night he cried for hours. In their shitty Motel 6 by the airport.

MARK: But his wife was there for him. No hottie models. Just her and her undying loyalty to him and love for him. Right by his side.

JAY: And they made love that night for the first time in years. And it was amazing. They stayed up all night.

MARK: Which is why she looks a little sick and why they're tired right now.

JAY: But that kiss he just gave her . . .

MARK: That's the sign of the birth of their new relationship.

JAY: Falling in love again. On their way back home.

(We both instinctually know we should stop here. And while the ending isn't the greatest or most realistic, we just really want them to win.)

III.

It is Sunday.

It is late summer 1991.

We are in our bedroom, clutching our acoustic guitars. We are tense. Afraid. Not at our best. We will be playing live at the Neutral Ground Coffee House tonight. They have recently opened, and this will be their first open-mic night. Anyone can sign up to perform three songs of their choosing. We plan to be there for our first-ever live performance together as an acoustic duo. We will go by the same name as the filmmaking duo we created a few years ago, the Duplass Brothers. Doors open at seven P.M.

It is almost five-thirty now.

And we are still working on our set list.

JAY: So we definitely open with "Mr. Black and Mrs. Brown."

("Mr. Black and Mrs. Brown" is an original that Jay has written. It is about two people who cannot see past their differences to find each other and consummate their true love. It is indisputably our best original song. We only have three original songs.)

MARK: One hundred percent. Then maybe hit 'em with something a little crowd-pleasing. That they know and can sing along to.

(We look at the list of potential cover songs. Mind you, these are not ironic. . . .)

"Sail On"—the Commodores
"A Horse with No Name"—America
"Stuck on You"—Lionel Richie
"Melissa"—the Allman Brothers Band
"Sara Smile"—Hall & Oates

JAY: How about "Stuck on You" right into "Sail On" to close?
MARK: I like the flow, but technically that's back-to-back Lionel Richie.
JAY: Good point.
MARK: Maybe "Sail On" second, and then we close with "B-Song"?

("B-Song" is another original.)

JAY: I just feel like "B-Song" is not our best.

(I wrote "B-Song," and I am oddly unfazed by Jay's criticism of it. Because Jay is right. I know it. And that there's what it is. This lack of ego in our process was evident very early.)

JAY: We should close with our best song.
MARK: "Mr. Black and Mrs. Brown" is our best song.
JAY: We gotta open with that, though.

MARK: Do we? I mean, think about it. That high harmony you do on the "He could not prove himself" line is kinda the emotional peak of the entire set. If we open with that, we might be sliding downhill for the rest of the performance.

(I have accidentally broken open the thinking that was previously locked. Jay immediately recognizes it with an excited high five. Again, no ego that he was not able to break it open himself. He quickly moves "Mr. Black and Mrs. Brown" to the set-closer position.)

JAY: Great call. "Sail On" second. "Mr. Black and Mrs. Brown" to close. And . . .

(Jay thinks for a second. And an idea hits.)

JAY: What if we open with "Everybody's Laughing."

(I am taken aback. It is a brand-new song that I wrote on my own. It is about a lesbian who goes into the woods at night and has sex with a ghost of herself because she is ashamed of her sexuality and worried people will laugh at her at school if she comes out. This song, written by a straight white fourteen-year-old male, is quite insufferable in many ways despite its beautiful, naïve heart.)

MARK: Really?
JAY: Yeah. It's our best after "Mr. Black and Mrs. Brown."
MARK: We haven't really worked out your part in it yet.
JAY: It'll be awesome. We'll wing it. Give it that "coming together in the moment" kinda energy.

(I accept Jay's opinion and leadership implicitly. This is how it is done with the Duplass Brothers in 1991.)

MARK: Love it. Let's do it.
JAY: Let's do it.

After our initial interest in filmmaking, we also became deeply obsessed with music. We felt that there was a fifty-fifty chance we'd become filmmakers or musicians. We saved our money from working summers at our Uncle Danny's family dry-cleaning business and bought ourselves two cheap acoustic guitars, a used drum kit, and a used four-track to record our demos. And tonight was turning out to be the culmination of all our hard work. Our first big gig. We arrived at the Neutral Ground at seven P.M., expecting a crowd snaking around the block.

Turned out we were the first ones to arrive. Also turned out that there were no microphones, PA system, or sound guy for tonight's open mic. Also turned out that the "stage" was covered with boxes of herbal tea and enormous plastic containers of weird concentrated iced coffee.

We asked the one volunteer employee what was happening with open-mic night tonight. He shrugged and said he hadn't heard anything about it. We checked the weekly entertainment mag. We had gotten the open-mic-night date correct. But it seemed that the Neutral Ground was still setting up shop and had somehow just forgotten about it.

We were crushed. Many of our friends were on their way to see us perform. We picked up our guitars and dragged ourselves back to our mom's Ford Explorer. We hopped in, but we didn't leave.

JAY: This sucks.

MARK: This *fucking* sucks.

JAY: It's just . . . demoralizing.

MARK: Should we just put a sign on the door for our friends?

JAY: We can't just leave.

MARK: I can't go back in there. I'm . . . I think I'm depressed.

(*Jay thinks this over. He looks at me and takes me in. I am already taller than him, but he will always be my older brother. Always the leader. And he can tell I need him right now.*)

JAY: We're not gonna play three songs for open-mic night tonight.

MARK: Dude, I know.

JAY: We're gonna play a full set.

(*There is something in the way Jay is looking at me now. I am deeply in tune with him. A surge is coming. It feels epic somehow.*)

JAY: We're going to clear that stage. We're going to set up with no mics, no PA system. And when our friends show up, we're gonna play every song we can come up with. Live. Raw. Just, like . . . us. Like . . . doing it.

(*I am overcome with inspiration. I smile with pride and excitement. I immediately pull out the set list and start adding song after song. Jay chimes in. The order comes together in a whirlwind of pump and inspiration. When it is done, it is a list of eleven songs. Four originals. Seven covers.*)

MARK: Are we doing this?
JAY: We are doing this!

We played our hearts out that night to a group of nine friends, one amazing older hippie dude named Les Jampole (who ended up being a bit of a musical mentor to us through the years of playing there), and an extremely disinterested volunteer employee. It was our first concert. And probably our best. Jay did what he had done so well for our entire relationship up to that point. He led me with the fearless confidence that was required of him. And he did it with a maturity and love way beyond his eighteen years. That night solidified for us both that, together, we might be able to accomplish anything. But perhaps more important, that Jay could always be counted on to lead us through the tough times. And that this brotherly dynamic was now fully cemented and would never change.

Two weeks later Jay left for college. Within a month of arriving, he had an emotional breakdown, and our brotherly dynamic completely changed.

SOME THOUGHTS ON

COMPROMISE

THE ART OF compromise is one of the hardest things we've
had to learn over the years. It's tricky. Really tricky. And it
keeps changing. How we relate, how we avoid pushing each
other's fussy buttons. How we get what we need to feel good
about ourselves but also give in enough to be respectful of the
other. It's a huge pain in the ass, but it's rewarding when we
get it right. So, a few thoughts . . .

CHECK YOUR EGO AT THE DOOR

When you're working closely with someone, it's natural to
want to be the "better" one. But this is a nasty impulse. Don't
give in to this one. Jay and I have come to accept that not only
does each of us have his own strengths, but there are also
certain days where one of us is more "on" than the other, and
this dynamic has to be okay. For instance, I have a real knack
for moving quickly and brashly through the early phases of
the creative process. From banging out a vomit draft of a
script to putting together a project's basic production structure to creating a pitch . . . I can get something on its feet,
quickly, that doesn't suck. What I have trouble with is closing.

But Jay is a master closer. You give him something between fifty and eighty percent done and he can drive that sucker home via his tremendous attention to detail and sheer force of will. And let's be clear: I am intimidated by Jay's closing power, and Jay is intimidated by my building power. This is a hard thing to accept at times but ultimately a very good thing. The more we joke about this, praise each other's strengths, laugh at each other's weaknesses, the better our work product becomes and the better our vibe together is. *But*—here's the hard part—sometimes one of us is just better at *both* things on a given day. That can be due to the state of burnout, how much sleep we've gotten, or just the luck of that day's brain chemistry. And you have to recognize it and let go of the thing that you are supposed to be good at if your collaborator is beating you at it on a given day. You have to. Or the product will suffer, and your relationship with your collaborator will suffer even more.

MAKE SOME PRESET RULES FOR THE DREADED IMPASSE

There will inevitably come a time when you and your collaborator will get to the place where neither of you is going to budge. We have accepted that in this place, neither person should be expected to act rationally and generously. Gridlock is gridlock is gridlock. So set your rules ahead of time about how to handle this kind of an impasse so you don't have to make rules *while* you're in gridlock mode. For us, impasse involves a basic two-part process. If the decision can be made by letting each have his way as an option for later, that's the best path. For instance, if we are shooting a scene and disagree about how a certain element should be performed or shot, we will film both versions. Usually time tells us which one is better after we have cooled down and gotten some perspective in the edit room. But there are also times when we are in the edit room deciding which song should roll over the credits. For instance, I might think it needs to push the emotion and play against the final comedic beat. Jay might feel that choice is too cheesy and we need to lie back and be more subtle. And we can't submit two versions of a TV episode to our network. So . . . how do we decide? Take a note from Regis Philbin and phone a friend. Bring in a group of your most trusted collaborators (co-workers, but also peers who do what you do and can give you advice). Show them both versions, without making a case for which one you personally prefer, and ninety-nine times out of a hundred the better version will prevail.

But (I know, a second "but") if it still is not clear, we have another way to settle it. . . .

PASSION IS KING

If all else fails, you should know your collaborator and yourself well enough to understand that there is a deep, soulful reason you are in a working relationship with this person. You should trust that their instincts are just as valid as your own, and after the dust settles you each should objectively be able to evaluate yourself and the person across from you and see who is more passionate about their case. It sounds like an arbitrary distinction, but we use this tactic quite often and it works very well. Whoever believes more deeply gets to win this one. And know that the next one that comes around will likely be yours.

PAY ATTENTION TO THE SIZE OF YOUR ENGINE

It took us about twenty-five "get your feelings hurt" sessions to figure this problem out. It's not easy to diagnose but it's an important one. Our creative brains work at different speeds and have different strengths. These aren't binary rules, but there are trends in the way we go about thinking and how we work, so it's important to take note and give your collaborator the respect they deserve. For instance, my head is like a bundle of fireworks. It goes off without warning and can be annoying, loud, and dangerous to those nearby. But it can also be fun. That said, Jay has discovered that when I am firing away, my brain can move so quickly and with such fervor that it doesn't allow Jay's ideas any space to collaborate with mine. So Jay has learned how to let the fireworks go off for a while until it's safe enough for him to get close and add his own ideas to the mix. Jay will be the first one to tell you how annoying it is, but in the end he knows he has to let me be me and obey my natural process.

On the flip side, Jay's ideas often come more slowly, in a more dreamlike fugue state. They usually take longer to develop, and they have a subtlety and sensitivity to them that can easily be trampled and smothered by my more brash and violent creative thought flow. So I have learned to shut up when Jay is birthing an idea, not trample all over it when my weird fireworks start going off, and give Jay the space he needs to let his ideas breathe and come to their resting place at his speed.

It may sound like a lot of work and compromise and restraint, and it is. But when it works, and my fire and Jay's precision come together on one big idea, it can be magical, and it makes the process truly worthwhile. You just have to set boundaries and get good at knowing yourself and your collaborator.

KNOW WHEN TO SAY WHEN

While some may argue that the greatest benefit to collaboration is that two heads are better than one, sometimes talking
about an idea with your collaborator can kill the magic. Sometimes you need to strike out on your own for a project or portion of a project in order to get it right. Don't be afraid to ask
for this. In our creative life, this has been a hard lesson to
learn. For instance, when Jay was writing a scene for our
movie *Cyrus* that was giving him trouble, I offered a way to fix
it that I thought was so obvious and Jay was just . . . resistant.
I kept intellectualizing with Jay as to why the fix I was offering
was the way to go, and it was baffling to me that he would not
accept it. Finally, Jay turned to me and said, "I know that's the
way to *fix* it, but I'm trying to do something different here,
and I don't know exactly what it is yet. I can't talk about it or
explain it, but I can *feel* it, and I need you to let me figure this
out on my own." It was a bummer moment for both of us, but
in the end Jay floundered around for a bit and then came up
with something that was not only as good as the fix I offered but
was a unique and inspired version of that fix and made the
script that much better for it.

Anyhow, the more we think about it, all of these ideas share
the same basic score: respecting and validating your creative
partner. Treating the relationship like a plant that needs
water, care, and a shit-ton of forgiveness to flourish.

And maybe some therapy.

Never underestimate the basic tools that you can get from a
few rounds with a good therapist.

TOP 10 FILMS OF ALL TIME (PART 2) *

We were pleased (though not altogether surprised) to discover that our individual Top 10 lists had quite a few crossover films. This was heartening. Our first step would be to compile both lists into one and simply remove the duplicate titles (*Rocky, American Movie, Raising Arizona, Dumb and Dumber*). This step immediately pared us down to sixteen films. From there things got tricky. How to get from sixteen to ten? We discussed and fairly quickly came up with a process of elimination via this simple question: "Which of these films can you simply not live with on our collective Top 10?" Our answers are boldfaced below.

American Movie

Raising Arizona

Same Time, Next Year (JD)

Tootsie

Rocky

Hoop Dreams

Margaret (MD)

The Crying Game

Dumb and Dumber

The Cruise

Starman (JD)

Henry Fool

The Horse Boy

The Black Stallion (MD)

You Can Count on Me

Close-Up

* *To be continued . . .*

IV.

"I'm the shortest person here. Including the girls."

"I don't think . . . I'm not sure that's . . . well, even if it's true, who cares?"

"I do. It's hard to meet people. There are so many people. This place is huge."

"It's not that huge."

"Mark, don't tell me that a school with fifty thousand students isn't huge."

(*Pause.*)

"Sorry. You're right. It is kinda huge."

"Thank you."

(*Then, a sneeze. Not from me. Or Mark. But from my room-mate Ed. Sleeping about four feet from where Mark and I are lying in my twin bed. Except we are not children anymore. I am a freshman in college. And I am having an incredibly hard time.*)

"Bless you, Ed."

(*A muffled "Thank you" emerges from underneath Ed's covers. He is nice enough to not be bothered by Mark's frequent overnight visits during this time. He is also nice enough to simply turn his back on us and not point out how utterly strange it is that two grown brothers are sleeping in one twin bed.*)

"Jay, if you want to just ditch it all and come home I don't think it's a bad thing."

"I do want to come home."

"Are you sure?"

(*Pause.*)

"No."

"Well, you have a month left of this semester. You can . . . ride it out and see how you feel after that?"

"Probably a good idea. I just . . ."

(*Pause.*)

(*I take my time here. I don't have the words for it. But it doesn't matter. This is the not the first time this conversation has happened. And Mark doesn't need the words to understand what I'm feeling. How I want to be grown-up enough to stand on my own. But how I also miss our tight-knit family and sense of security. How the thought of coming home feels beautiful but also like a failure. So instead I simply cry for a little bit into Mark's armpit. This moment does two things. First, it makes Ed even more uncomfortable. Second, it actually makes Mark feel good. That he can provide some*) *care and comfort for me, the person who has been doing that very thing for him, pretty much nonstop, since he was born.)*

Three months earlier, in the fall of 1991, I had left our home in Metairie to attend the University of Texas at Austin on a full scholarship. I was smart, responsible, and genuinely excited. I thought I'd be fine.

But within the first few weeks, my well-being became a major concern for my family. I began calling home more and more. I struggled with making friends and finding my way on such a huge college campus. While our mother wanted to comfort me, she couldn't bear to hear her son suffering, so she quickly became of little use on the phone. Our dad was a rock. He was full of smart, confidence-boosting advice for his first-born son. He did everything right. Yet in the long run, our dad's confidence and ability to see so clearly what the solutions were to my problems only made me feel worse for not being able to enact those solutions. I simply could not take myself out of the spiraling depression in which I found myself. When I spoke with our mom, I was aware that my suffering made her suffer twice as badly. Talking to Dad made me acutely aware that I was not as confident and well equipped to face the world as he was.

So I started asking for Mark when I called home . . . the nacho-eating, skater-banged, Iron Maiden–listening, prepubescent ball of confused hormones. And there was something in the reckless confidence of Mark's youth that was exactly what I needed.

And this is where the first big turn in our relationship came. As the long-distance phone bill skyrocketed, so did our closeness. And so did Mark's ability to make me laugh, loosen up, and remind me of that childlike confidence with which I had led Mark for so many years.

So, at age fourteen, Mark began taking cheap Southwest flights by himself on weekends to visit me in Austin. There, we would go see live music. Hang out in coffee shops and meet weird early-nineties Austin people. Take in every indie film that came through town. Mark would do keg stands at my friends' parties, and I would recklessly join in. We were a bit of a circus act of sorts that people wanted to get to know. My confidence started to rebuild itself and my social life started to grow. We met new people and did all kinds of new things (like smoke weed together for the first time) and began to dream about our futures together the way we did when we were little kids. It was a grand reconnection of the Duplass Brothers as we were before I left for college, but now Mark was ever so slightly in the lead, taking care of me for the first time. It was a dynamic that formed rather quickly but stuck for many years to come.

Perhaps the most important thing this period taught us was how wonderfully complex and shape-shifting relationships can be. Until that point we were certain that, because our relationship began a certain way, it would follow that dynamic forever. Instead we were forced to reexamine what it meant to be truly intimate with someone. That sometimes we would be required to be different things to each other. That we'd have to remain open to what the other one needed, allow him the space to change, and learn how to grow with him to accommodate those changes.

In short, we accidentally started learning way back in the early nineties how to become the husbands, fathers, and partners we ultimately wanted to be.

IN DEFENSE OF *THE KARATE KID PART II**

THERE ARE so many things wrong with this movie. Ralph Macchio is still playing a high school senior even though he's pushing thirty. Mr. Miyagi's formerly subtle, well-placed quips of wisdom from the first film are now a relentless barrage of New Agey self-help schmaltz. Daniel's new love interest is an Okinawan girl who takes his jokes literally, missing his already unfunny humor (but adding an unintended aura of borderline racism to the entire film!). The young villain is an inherently unthreatening individual who cackles at inopportune moments like a bipolar hyena. A former friend of Mr. Miyagi's named Sato speaks in an unintelligent guttural fiasco that can only be described as "evil guy voice." The best moments of the first film are overtly recycled, functioning less like fun callbacks and more like thinly disguised, sad approximations of their former selves. The plotting is generic. The music is pushed. The performances are stilted. The pacing is awful. This film is simply not good.

---

* We realize that we've already mentioned the *Karate Kid* movies twice and you're barely fifty pages into the book, so we just want to make it super clear that we're not overly obsessed with them. Our obsession is perfectly appropriate for our age range.

But there's a moment a little more than halfway through the film that has always fascinated us. One that we have revisited often throughout the years. It takes place just after the death of Mr. Miyagi's father. He is sitting by himself on a beach in one of the few simple, elegantly composed shots of the film. He occupies the left side of the frame. The right side is empty. As the score settles into a subtle, ambient position that suggests it will lay back over the next few minutes so as not to compete with an important moment, Daniel walks up and sits in the empty portion of the frame.

For the next few minutes, Ralph Macchio delivers a monologue about the time he lost his father. How it made him feel. His sense of regret for not telling his father more often that he loved him. But also how he believes, deep down, that his father understood how much Daniel did care for him. Even though he didn't say it enough. And that Daniel has learned to be okay with this. The score lays back in all the right ways. The monologue is a nuanced wave of elegant restraint and raw emotion. Ralph nails it with a naturalistic display of loving support for his friend, appropriately colored by his own personal remorse. Even the wind seems to kick up at all the right moments, as if the universe is itself a collaborator in this epic cinematic moment. And as Daniel nears the end of his speech, you can't take your eyes off of him. Until you do. Because you soon notice that Mr. Miyagi's lips are beginning to quiver. And his eyes are welling with tears. And Daniel sees it too! And he feeds on it as he nears the climax of his story! They work together like the perfect team! The chemistry is impeccable! And the tears may not hold. But the lips outright tremble now! As Daniel finishes his story, he reaches out for his friend's shoulder, and just at the moment . . . a single tear falls down the right side of Mr. Miyagi's face. The score peaks. The wind dies down. The scene ends.

What. The. Fuck.

How did that happen? Like a golden cloak shimmering in the midst of a veritable sea of dog shit, this utterly perfect scene emerges from the cesspool that is *The Karate Kid Part II.* And all of our snark . . . all of our judgment . . . all of our criticisms of the movie . . . they are at once all thrown back in our faces. And we are forced to eat the very shit that we once threw. Because we cry with this film now. Genuinely moved by it. And shocked that a moment of such greatness can occur in a vacuum.

Mostly, though, we are humbled. And we remember that making a decent piece of art is incredibly difficult. It requires every possible skill set you can muster, and then it requires a lot of luck on top of that. So every time we hear Peter Cetera's over-the-top theme song, we remember that *The Karate Kid Part II* is simply trying to be "the man who will fight for our honor." We remember that this fight is a noble one in and of itself. So we try on a little respect. We let the snarky criticism go. And we celebrate the wonderful four minutes that this bizarre, confusing film gifted to us.

HOUSING

WE ASKED SOME of our good friends what they wanted us to write about in this book. Nick Kroll came back and said he appreciated how we always seemed to harbor these weirdly researched pockets of "dork wisdom" that he has found useful over the years. That we were artists who also had these bizarrely old-school, pragmatic approaches to life's problems. So, thanks to Nick Kroll, you are going to get some unsolicited, dorky advice. If you don't like these bronze nuggets of wisdom, feel free to tweet a picture of dog shit at Nick Kroll now. But if you're interested, keep reading.

Let's say you are an artist who likes to make weird art that probably won't make money. If this is you, we love you. Or you're an inventor of odd ideas, or a start-up that is not guaranteed to work. If this is you, we need you. You're awesome. But your road could be hard. And you need to be able to live cheaply until you "hit" (or maybe live cheaply forever). So you need a smart plan. You need to guarantee that you have as much time as possible to make your real work instead of dying a slow creative death in a crappy day job in order to pay your outlandish living expenses. To this end, here are a few tips:

1) While you are woodshedding and developing your craft, do not live in a big city with expensive rents. Find a place like Detroit or New Orleans, even the outskirts of Portland and Austin. These places offer a community of creative, smart young underdogs chasing their dreams, with affordable housing to boot. Live here until you need to live in one of the major markets (which is maybe never, by the way).

2) Buy a house in this place as soon as possible. We realize that this sounds insanely difficult, but you can buy a home in the up-and-coming areas of Detroit and New Orleans for less than $50,000. Not to get all math dork up in here, but that means all you need to do is save up (or charge to a willing credit card) $5,000 for a ten percent down payment. Then your total mortgage, with taxes-insurance-upkeep, will likely be less than $750 a month. We know, $750 a month can be a lot. So . . .

3) Get yourself some roommates to help cover the monthly bill. They can even pay you some advance rent to help with the down payment. Also, this roommate portion is just as important for community as it is for money. When you are young, you need people who know you and understand you to bounce your ideas off of. We have lived in houses with up to five people at a time, and it was invaluable to our developmental and creative process. Yes, the bathroom was nasty and the kitchen was roach-heavy, but it was worth it. Not to mention, if you can rent out two to three bedrooms in this home for $300 to $400 month, you will have your

entire mortgage paid for (with maybe even a little rice-and-beans stipend left over) and will be living rent-free.

4) Make sure the neighborhood where you buy has at least a few artists living there. Invite other artists to live with you and near you. Build a community around you, and as the cool factor rises (we know, dorky), so will the value of your home. Soon enough, you will have a huge home-equity stake in a neighborhood that has risen in value, and you will actually make money refinancing your home.

5) This is the most important part. When you are hitting it big and don't need this house anymore, please just hold on to it and rent it *very* cheaply to your roommates who have not yet broken out. They need your help, and you can give them that help now. And you should.

How'd we do, Nicky?

V.

When I turned fifteen and got my driver's license, it was all over. My life as a high school freshman ended and my life as a de facto college student began. Every chance I got I would hop into the car and drive eight hours to Austin for extended weekend visits to see Jay. As long as I made my grades, our parents were supportive of the absences. And though it was clearly unorthodox, the family dynamic seemed to be working. Jay's confidence was returning, and he and I were reconnected and as close as ever.

As far as Jay and I were concerned, this was the time frame when we truly fell in love as collaborators. It was then that we became the inseparable soul mates that we always wanted to be. And being in Austin, which was full of great self-made artists in the early nineties, was a big part of it. From musicians like Daniel Johnston and Joe Rockhead to indie filmmaker heroes like Richard Linklater and Robert Rodriguez, we always had things to see and people to look up to. We would see Linklater give Q&A talkbacks at midnight screenings of *Slacker* at the Dobie Theater. He wore jeans and ratty T-shirts and old Nikes. He felt like a regular dude. Could he possibly be making important art films without a beret *or* a turtleneck? It seemed so. He made us believe that maybe we could actually be successful filmmakers too. And we continued dreaming together about who we could become.

Summers during this period were a particularly glorious time. Jay would come home from school and I would be anxiously waiting with my acoustic guitar and our parents' crappy video camera. Three months of living back in the suburbs, the world whatever we wanted it to be. We would work some sort of odd job during the day (landscaping crews, bussing tables, our uncle's dry cleaner's), but the nights were when we shined. We would record cover versions of our favorite Commodores and Lionel Richie songs on our used four-track. We'd go for three-mile runs in the middle of the night. We'd take the video camera and film ourselves jumping trains, trying to improvise a narrative and failing terribly. Then come home and use our guitars to live-score whatever dumb footage we'd shot until the sun came up. Then we'd jump into the pool, listen to late-album Steely Dan, sleep a few hours, and do it all over again. These were some of the happiest times in our lives. We still didn't believe we would actually become successful artists, but we were playing house in a way. Pretending to live the lives of Donald Fagen and Walter Becker of Steely Dan. Or the Coen Brothers. We threw ourselves into each other, distancing ourselves a bit from our friends, our girlfriends, and even our parents.

By the time my senior year of high school came around, I was faced with a decision to pay full tuition at UC Berkeley and build my own life out in California or take a full-ride scholarship to UT Austin like Jay did. It should have been a very difficult decision. But it wasn't. The thought of not being with Jay felt, quite simply, like a divorce. I still don't know if it was healthy. But it was what it was.

So in 1995 I moved to Austin to attend the University of
Texas as well, and by the time I arrived the new brother dynamic was squarely in place. Jay wasn't the leader anymore,
and I wasn't the follower. We were more like peers. Almost
like twins. We could finish each other's sentences, we shared
the exact same tastes. We could spend hours on end together,
never tiring of each other's company, never fighting. The only
real issue we had was our constant discussion of whether we
should be pursuing movies or music as a career and whether
we were doing ourselves a disservice by trying to pursue both
simultaneously. And with Jay's impending graduation from
UT, we both had the feeling that "shit just got real." That it was
time to figure out how to make a living and see if this artist's
life was a possible reality. At the time, I had a slight lean
toward music and Jay toward film. He would play in my bands,
but I was more of the leader there. Meanwhile, we were discussing ways that Jay could make money as a recent college
graduate. So we devised a scheme. I needed a conversion van
with a foldout bed to go touring, as I was pursuing a solo
singer-songwriter career at the time. (Yes, I had sideburns
and a soul patch. And Tevas.) And we decided that, since we'd
both learned how to edit movies in film school, we would buy
an editing machine and start an editing business. Jay could be
the leader of that side of our collaboration, make his living,
and learn more about filmmaking in the process.

We sold both of our cars, pooled our money, and scraped
together enough to buy me a shitty van and also the baseline
Avid computer to start our editing business. We rented an office from a friend for $100 a month (a box with no windows),
and in 1997 we officially started Duplass Brothers Produc-
tions. The company released my first solo album, a thousand

pressed CDs that I sold from the back of my van on my self-booked tours, and we edited all the low-budget features being made in Austin at the time at the cool rate of $15 an hour.

We didn't realize it at the time, but a tiny shift was occurring. One that was very important to the future of our careers. We were, ever so slightly, moving away from the "we are one person" way of operating and into the area that we now call "president and vice president" mode, whereby one of us leads ever so slightly on a given discipline or project. (More on this later.)

And we functioned like this for quite a few years. Jay played with me in my music projects when he could, and I edited with the business when I wasn't on tour. It was an unusual separation for us, but it worked well and allowed us to have a bit of space while still working together. Still, success was not coming in either field, and we were wondering where we would end up. In the back of our minds, both of us were thinking that we'd probably have to give up soon and try to get into some sort of graduate school and ultimately find real jobs. After all, the touring was barely enough to get by, and the editing business was barely turning a profit. Times were tight even for our less-than-$250-a-month rents. (To save cash, we lived on the outskirts of town in shitty apartments with too many roommates.)

Eventually a huge opportunity fell into our laps. Through a high school friend connection, a former Fortune 500 start-up hired us to make a documentary about their company. They apologized for the "small budget," offering us half a million dollars to make it. We tried not to excitement-vomit in their faces in the meeting. But when we left we danced in the alleyway behind the building, punching and slapping each other with unbridled joy. The project would be a perfect fit for us. I would create the music score, Jay would do the on-the-ground filming, and we would edit it together along with our new employee, Jay Deuby (who would eventually become our longtime collaborator and unofficial third brother).

We ultimately made the film incredibly cheaply, which allowed us to pay our friends and collaborators extraordinarily well and still pocket a large chunk of cash ourselves. And, in a moment of great irony, just as we handed the film over to them, the dot-com bubble burst and the company folded. No one ever saw the film.

But we didn't care. We were twenty-two and twenty-six. For the first time in our lives, we had some real money in our bank accounts. Money we had made as "artists." We talked and talked into the night about what we should do with it. A big part of us wanted to invest the money. Or even buy a house. We knew that artists had to save, that when the cash came in you had to be smart and put it aside for the dry spells. But, again, we were twenty-two and twenty-six. And we were dreaming big. So even though we had yet to write and direct any kind of narrative film (even a short) that was remotely watchable, we decided to use our profits from the documentary to make our first narrative feature film. We wanted to be Linklater and Rodriguez. We wanted to go for it.

Within six months we were in preproduction on *Vince Del Rio*.

GIRLFRIENDS

IF THERE WAS ever a heyday of our brotherly connection, it was during our time in Austin. Once we were back together in the same place we were like a couple reunited after World War II. Okay, not really. But we were dorky, we were excited, and we were soul mates.

It was also during this time that we both were embarking on long-term romantic relationships. Jay met his girlfriend senior year, and I met mine freshman year (we will hold back the names to protect the innocent). These two amazing women were somehow able to look past Jay's sideburns and my hemp necklaces, and both couples quickly became fairly serious. Jay's girlfriend was roughly the same age as me and my girlfriend, so the chemistry worked pretty well for us as a foursome. And, in truth, in all the time we were dating there were very few conflicts, considering how close Jay and I were and the potential for disaster awaiting all of us in that four-way soup. But looking back on it now, we can see how unhealthy it all was.

First of all, we had no idea how to respect the privacy of a romantic relationship. Whatever was happening behind closed doors with our girlfriends was immediately opened up for brotherly conversation and analysis. Some of the things we shared were downright disrespectful, but we had no clue that this was inappropriate in any way because we were soul mates and we shared everything. The endgame of this was simple . . . no matter how close we got to our girlfriends, there was no way it could compare to the closeness that we shared as brothers. And while we sensed something was off in the way we were relating to our girlfriends at the time, we couldn't quite put our finger on it. In all honesty, these were fantastic women we were dating. We were both lucky to have them choose us. But there was a barrier there. And neither of us could truly see through the present to any potential long-term future with them. Part of it was that we were still young and a bit immature, but there was also something much deeper and more dysfunctional at work. We didn't realize what it was until we had a conversation one day with a set of identical twins who were regaling us with tales of what they described as their "hopelessly fucked-up love lives." They had recently decided that they weren't going to date anyone who was not also a twin. Their theory was that no one could understand that specific bond that they shared with their twin unless they were also a twin. Anyone else that they tried to date would always feel threatened and never understand that, no matter what, no one would ever be as close to them as their twin sibling.

This conversation hit us like a lightning bolt. And we immediately understood what was happening. We had been dating our girlfriends for a few years, but the relationships had stopped progressing. And it was most certainly due to the level of closeness that we shared as brothers. At the end of the day, we shared our deepest and darkest secrets with each other and not our girlfriends. When we needed a shoulder, we turned to each other. And not them.

Kinda sweet.

Kinda fucked up.

In the end, our graduations came and we all went our separate ways. I went on tour, Jay stayed back with the editing business, and our foursome that had so much potential broke up. It was a sad time, and we both felt a bit soul-sick about the way things ended in our first grown-up romantic relationships.

In the middle of the tour I had a short break, so Jay flew out to meet me in Las Vegas for a few days. Jay brought with him two vintage pastel suits and two Hawaiian shirts. We dressed up like late-seventies tourists and roamed the streets of Vegas. We took stupid pictures, we got onstage with a low-rent casino's house band and played a tight version of Toto's "Africa" with them. I talked about the loneliness of touring and Jay talked about his fears about making our upcoming first feature film. It was a beautiful but bittersweet couple of days. It reconfirmed how strong our bond was, how even at this somewhat awkward time in our lives our simply being together could raise our spirits and make us stronger. But we could also feel the dysfunction of our closeness. That our union was most likely the reason things didn't work out with our ex-girlfriends. That we might never find anyone we could be as close with as we were with each other. That, quite frankly, we might end up in Vegas thirty years from now wearing these suits and doing all the ridiculous things we were currently doing, but without a hint of irony. And that was a really fucking scary thought.

It wasn't until much later, when we finally met the women we would eventually marry, that we learned a much harder truth about all of this. That we would somehow have to create space inside our bizarre order of the brotherhood to make room for successful romantic relationships to grow.

EIGHTY IS ENOUGH

WHILE WE OBVIOUSLY collaborate as brothers quite a bit, the truth is we work with a much larger group of people on a weekly if not daily basis. And we've come to understand that this large group of friends and colleagues with whom we collaborate is an integral part of our process.

We often get asked how we make so many projects in a year. All false modesty aside, our output can be pretty bananas; this year alone we'll make multiple indie films, a few TV shows, some international commercials; we'll engage in multiple acting roles, finish a couple of studio writing assignments, write this book, etc. It all adds up and seems like a lot if you think of two brothers trying to crank all of this out on their own. So . . . how do we do it? Well, one answer is that we have a fundamental desperation to make things, and we are willing to destroy ourselves to get those things done (more on this extremely helpful-dangerous element of our personalities later on). But the simplest answer is that we don't make all of these projects on our own. In fact, we don't make any of them on our own. And part of the reason for this is time constraints, but mostly it has to do with an ideology we have developed over the years about what it means to be an "original" artist.

For a while, we thought we wanted to be *auteurs*. This is a dangerous and, quite frankly, stupid word. In our opinion, most of the bad films we see come from people being close-minded and unwilling to compromise their "vision" of a project. To be clear, some people really can visualize a piece of art and see it through and, somehow, make it great. It seems that people like the Coen Brothers have a specific vision of what their movies will look like from the moment they begin writing them, and then somehow are able to realize that vision and make those movies, for the most part, inspired and impeccably amazing. We, however, are not the Coen Brothers. We tried that approach once and we failed miserably (more on this later as well). We have realized that we are in fact human beings who are good at some things and not so good at other things. We are capable of being right and wrong at any given turn in the creative process, and we need help from the smart people around us to be the best versions of ourselves we can be.

And this is why we have implemented the "Eighty is enough" approach to making films, partly an homage to the fantastic Dick Van Patten television show of the early 1980s but mostly a theory that has resulted in years of us failing at making decent art, eating crow, and finding smart people nearby to bail us out. In other words, try your best to get your work at any given stage to what you think is at least eighty percent as good as it can be. Then, when you hit a wall, share it with someone you trust and see how it can be improved.

Let's say we have an idea for a movie. The two of us will spend a ton of time talking it over, coming up with scene ideas, hammering the characters and plot into somewhat legible shape. Then we tend to go off and begin the oral story-telling phase. At dinner parties, over lunch, while taking walks with friends, etc., we begin to tell the story to people. Inevitably, we will look into their eyes and see where their interest piques and where it wanes. And when it wanes, we just ask them how they felt, what they liked, and what they wanted more or less of in the story.

After a few rounds of this, the two of us will put together a written outline for the film. Again, we hammer it until it's about eighty percent there (or roughly as far as we can take it until we lose perspective and risk making changes that might actually ruin it). At this point, since it's only a few pages, we will share it with quite a few writers and also with one person who does not work in the film business whatsoever. It's not a huge time ask, and if we're lucky the multiple feedbacks will dovetail in a way that tells us what's missing. Sometimes everyone agrees and it's easy. Sometimes the feedback is more disparate. Our job is to figure out what makes the most sense and, often, to find what people call the "note behind the note"; i.e., sometimes people say they want "less of this character" when they really just want more of another character. This phase can be a little confusing, but ultimately we take that feedback and adjust our outline.

Now it's time to write the script. This part sucks. It's hard. It's grueling. But we are always encouraged to finish because we already have a scene-by-scene outline that has been pretty well vetted by some of our smartest peers. And when that draft is done, we ping-pong it between just the two of us until it's at that terrible place where you ask yourself "Are we making it better? Worse? Same?" When you get here, you're probably close to eighty percent again, and it's time to bring in the big guns. This is when we call in one or two great writers and one more smart, nonindustry person to read the draft. It's a big ask, so you should always be prepared to return the favor.

But in our opinion this is the most critical part of the process. You will be feeling defensive of your script. Because you have worked so hard on it. But you have to check your ego at the door and listen to what is landing and what is not landing. We have had our egos beaten out of us because we now realize that we don't always know what's best for our movie at every step of the creative process. And this is where the *auteur* gets into trouble. In our opinion, if you hear a consistent note or complaint about your script and ignore it, you are likely headed for heartbreak. You are likely ignoring something you missed and that could quite possibly sink your movie. All because you are afraid to admit you don't know everything about making movies? Who the fuck does? Okay, fine, the Coen Brothers. But still. Who else? We've come to believe, right or wrong, that it doesn't make us any less valuable as filmmakers to admit we get stuck, we need help, we're not as smart as we want to be, and our friends help us become better.

And this process holds true for shooting the film and editing it as well. We often hold screenings for up to forty people to watch rough cuts of our projects. And we ask extremely difficult questions about what they like and don't like. And it can be very unpleasant, but our movies and TV shows always improve when we invite other people into the process.

This is not to say that we are celebrating our own mediocrity. We occasionally get truly inspired and are able to take a movie much further than that eighty percent level on our own, but we feel it's important to know that just because you aren't the Coen Brothers doesn't mean you can't put together a fantastic film. You just need to drop your ego sometimes and let everyone stomp all over it for a little bit. They'll inevitably pick you back up and dust you off when your film is great. And it will all be worth it. Trust us on this one.

AIRPORT

#2

(Seated directly across from us in the Austin-Bergstrom Airport is a man in his late forties to early fifties. He wears tan slacks and a muted-patterned, short-sleeved button-down. His hair is neatly combed and cut short. He is balding up the middle but not yet fully gray. He holds a small briefcase in his lap. He looks off to his left at nothing in particular. He feels like a Midwesterner, maybe. His face is kind. His hands are small. He doesn't look like he could hurt a fly.)

JAY: So the movie is called *The Murderer*.
MARK: Yep. Starring him.
JAY: One hundred percent.

(The man does not flinch. For some reason his utter stillness makes us giggle.)

MARK: I mean, this still frame from right here could literally be the poster.
JAY: Make it black and white. Big-ass thick font underneath him.
MARK: Like *The Pawnbroker*.
JAY: But more real.

(We watch him for a moment, both of us trying to think of an interesting plot.)

MARK: It's like he's one of those guys who has more patience than you could possibly imagine having.

JAY: He has like six highly opinionated daughters and one son, who hates him for no apparent reason.

(Giggling.)

JAY: And they and his wife just rule his ass.

MARK: And he takes it. Lovingly. Almost as if he . . . really enjoys it.

JAY: Everyone who knows him is just, like, "How does Gene do it? Salt of the earth."

MARK: "He's just one of those guys that was born a pure heart."

(Pause.)

JAY: *(smiling)* But not everybody sees him that way. Some people say there's no way anyone is that nice.

MARK: Right. Like . . . he has to have some kind of . . . secret outlet.

JAY: In the middle of the night.

MARK: Ha! Yes. Gene gets up in the middle of the night, goes into his backyard when everyone else is asleep, and just fuckin' . . .

JAY: Strangles a bunch of squirrels.

(Here, Mark bursts out laughing. I love that I can still make him laugh like that. But I realize I must keep it down, lest

"Gene" turn his murderous instincts upon us in this very air-port.)

MARK: He's in the Squirrel Killers Club.
JAY: He's the fucking president!

(We laugh a bit more at this. Then it fades.)

MARK: Love this character.
JAY: But what's the story?

(Thinking. As this happens, "Gene" fiddles with his nose a bit. Not a booger pick. Just an itch. But something about it is a touch darker. Subtle. But there.)

MARK: Everything was fine for Gene until he took his family to New Orleans for Mardi Gras.
JAY: Which was a big mistake?
MARK: Cuz the six girls were all growing up. And getting gorgeous. And that city during Mardi Gras is just . . .
JAY: It can be dangerous for out-of-towners.
MARK: Right. But Gene is used to letting the family lead him around. And, sure enough, they ended up in a shady part of town where tourists just shouldn't go.
JAY: This is really good, by the way. I'm gonna shut up. You keep going.
MARK: Thanks. So this somewhat unhinged lady walks up to them and asks for some money. And when they try to keep walking, she reaches out for one of Gene's middle daughters. And something just . . . snaps.
JAY: In Gene?

MARK: In Gene. And he pummels the ever-living shit out of this woman. Right in front of his family.

JAY: Oh shit. Like . . . the most violent thing you've ever seen.

MARK: Uh-huh. Smashing her face into the sidewalk, over and over again.

JAY: Blood everywhere.

MARK: And before Gene knows it, she is no longer resisting.

JAY: And the family is utterly quiet.

MARK: He's sweating. Breathless. Staring down at the somewhat frail drug addict at his feet.

JAY: And she is . . .

(We both look at each other. Do we want to take it here?)

MARK: She's dead.

(We both look at "Gene" now and watch him, thinking of him as a man who has killed someone. Everything changes. His entire context and vibe. It's eerie. But exciting too.)

JAY: It was technically self-defense.

MARK: Yep. The cops come. They tell the story. . . .

JAY: Luckily there was a knife in her pocket—

MARK: Ooh, that's good. Justifiable homicide and self-defense. So he doesn't even get arrested.

JAY: And they go back home the next day to return to life as normal.

MARK: But they can't. Everything has changed.

JAY: Because they are living with a man who is capable of murder.

MARK: And they can't just order him around anymore. They are almost . . . scared of him.

JAY: And he misses his old life. He misses being ruled by his insensitive family. And his ability to be patient starts to wane.
MARK: Oh shit.
JAY: Uh-huh. And he starts to take kickboxing classes.
MARK: Dude, I wanna make this movie.
JAY: I do too!
MARK: It's like . . . all the great stuff from *A History of Violence* and then it spins out into some sort of weird, like . . .
JAY: Scandinavian character study.
MARK: Yes! Pulpy Lars von Trier!
JAY: So good.

(We laugh for a bit and then get quiet. Thinking.)

MARK: How does it end?
JAY: I don't know.
MARK: Me neither.

(And now we watch him a bit more just staring off into space. Wondering what he could be thinking about. Projecting deep, dark things onto his formerly sweet disposition.)

VI.

IN LATE 2000 we pulled together $65,000 from our corporate documentary salary (almost all of our savings) and launched into the script for *Vince Del Rio,* our first feature film. We decided on a story about a former standout high school cross-country runner (played by Mark) from the Texas border town of Del Rio. This runner, Vince, cheats in an Olympic Trials qualifying race and lands a spot in the actual Olympic Trials. It was inspired by our deep love of the original *Rocky* film. About a man who gets a fluke shot at redemption and greatness.

Mark, who was working primarily as a touring musician at the time, came off the road to get into fantastic running shape for the film and, along with me and our other close collaborator and editor, Jay Deuby, wrote the script that I would direct. In a few months, we had a draft that we felt was in good shape and set a date to shoot the film in early summer 2001.

During the Christmas holidays of 2000, we went back to our parents' home in New Orleans and made a practice short film for fun. It was about a guy (again, Mark) who breaks up with his girlfriend and travels across the country to get her back. It was made for no money with a cast and crew of three people, most of whom had never worked on a movie before. It was improvised, goofy, a little funny, and definitely felt more like "us" than a film about a runner from the Texas border. But we weren't thinking about that at the time. We put that little short film away without editing it and turned back to prep for *Vince Del Rio*. Our magnum opus.

The next day we went into a densely wooded levee area near our childhood home and shot some test footage of Mark running around as the character of Vince Del Rio. It was a pure white cloudy winter day, and my camera lost Mark quite a bit in the fog, zooming in and out to find him. I shot it on our parents' lo-fi one-chip DV camera, which is technical jargon for "a piece of shit." The shoot felt like a bust.

When we got home and watched the footage, however, there was a certain magic to it. The grain, the fog, the zooms. It felt raw, inspired, and unique. We got so excited we could barely contain ourselves.

"If it looks this good with just the two of us shooting it on a crappy camera, just think how awesome it will be when we shoot this movie with pro cameras and a full professional crew, with that great Texas summer light and heat!"

When summer rolled around, we lucked out by getting a more experienced crew than the meager salaries we could afford actually deserved. These were veteran players who had been on pro film sets, and we were blessed to have them. We hired all the right positions and headed to South Texas for our four-week shoot.

Before we left, we read as many books on filmmaking as we could get our hands on. We wanted to get all the terminology and lingo right. We wanted to make sure we knew all the union rules so we'd appear experienced and in charge. We were obsessed with leading a tightly run, professional shoot despite our relatively small budget and extreme inexperience.

And, as it turned out, we were very good at that aspect of filmmaking. Being good Catholic boys, we listened to our producers and assistant directors and we perfectly followed the schedule and protocol. We never went over our allotted shoot hours. Not once. We came in on time and on budget every day. People were loving how efficient and confident we were. Whenever they asked us "Did you get it?" regarding a particular take, we turned with a confident thumbs-up and moved on so we could "make our day," as they call it. It was hard work, but we felt great and everyone loved us so much. We never knew making a film could be so much fun and, honestly, so easy.

When the shoot was done, word spread around Austin how nice, awesome, and professional The Boys were. We went into the editing suite immediately and started putting it together. And that is when we started to get a growing feeling of trouble.

The first thing we noticed was that there wasn't much of that "magic" we were hoping for in the footage. This realization didn't rock us to our core, but we couldn't help remembering the feeling we'd had that previous Christmas when we watched the aborted test running footage from the levee in New Orleans. The rawness, the life in it. But we powered ahead and waited to watch a full cut before making any judgments.

And that's when we started to panic. When we watched the first cut together, we realized that something was deeply wrong with the movie. And the worst part was that we couldn't define the problem. It was beautifully shot. The production design was elegant. The performances were not stellar, but they were fine. And the story itself was being conveyed in a clear manner. Yet the whole movie was just kind of . . . blah. Being inexperienced filmmakers, we wondered if we were just sick of our movie and maybe this thing really was great! (NOTE: If you are ever wondering this same thing, chances are your movie isn't great. Sorry.)

So we decided to hold a test screening for about fifty friends and local filmmakers to see how it played. And that's when we knew. Even before the film ended. *Vince Del Rio* was dead. We could feel it in the room. See it on people's faces. They were all sitting there thinking the same thing: "It's not *bad,* it's just not really *anything.*" Our friends stayed and gave us their most polite feedback, and we dragged ourselves back to the office to decide what to do.

We could try to salvage the film with rewrites and reshoots. Really dig in and see what we could do to make it better. But how? We'd thought what we were shooting *last* time was good. Who was to say that we wouldn't go back and just shoot more bad footage? We felt lost and incapable of understanding why the movie wasn't working, much less what would actually improve the film. The more we talked about it, the more we realized that *Vince Del Rio* was endemically flawed to its core and we were in no position to be able to save it. Not wanting to throw good money and effort after bad, we decided to bury the film. We had to call everyone who had worked on it and explain what had happened. We watched our bank accounts drain of all the money we had made on our big corporate documentary six months earlier. We were now twenty-four and twenty-eight. We were pretty much broke. And we were beginning to realize that our dreams were probably not going to happen for us.

SOME THOUGHTS ON
ARGUING

THERE IS NO way to avoid arguing. It seems to be something most people just accept and spend very little time working on ways to improve. Arguing can be a good thing (in the long run). However, we all tend to suck at it to varying degrees, depending on our current level of insecurity, history of the subject matter, lack of sleep, etc. While we by no means have the answers for arguing successfully with our spouses, we have found a few tricks that can be helpful while navigating the confusing jungle of trying to win an argument and also trying to continue a healthy relationship with your partner.

I) There is one magic bullet that can nip any argument in the bud. If used successfully, this tactic can tell you whether this argument contains an actual issue that needs discussing or whether it's just a fleeting moment of fussiness that should simply be pushed aside. It's called the Porky Principle. One of you (usually the one who is less pissed off) needs to scream "Porky Pig!" as quickly as possible when the argument starts. When this is called out, you both need to take your pants off. And your underwear. But leave your tops on (i.e., the Porky Pig look). If you have a hard time taking the argument seriously with this new look of yours and your partner's, that's a good thing. If you laugh, that's even better. That usually means this was a fleeting moment of fussiness. Enjoy the laughter. Let the issue go. And put your pants back on. Or, if so inclined, take your tops off and go for the makeup sex. If, however, one (or both) of you is too angry or stubborn to let go of the argument, that's cool too. It just means you have to get into it.

2) For fuck's sake learn how to validate the other one's opinion before you shut them down with your own. This took us about thirty-five years to learn. It's so simple. Yet people rarely do this. Yes, we all want to win the argument and get our way. Or defend ourselves from an attack. Whatever the case may be, listening to someone's argument and letting them know you understand their position does nothing to diminish your own position. In fact, it only makes your position stronger. Because, if you don't let that person know that you've heard them, they will continue to blast you with their argument and won't even be able to hear yours until they have felt heard. So even if you are feeling wronged and that your significant other is in a crazed state of stupidity . . . hear their side, don't interrupt, and let them know that you have heard them and understood them. Then make your case. We promise you (from years of doing this poorly) that this will expedite and improve the argument's outcome. We all just want to be heard and understood.

3) Simple, but effective: IMPOSE A CURFEW. No serious arguments about long-term ongoing issues after bedtime. If it's a small and timely issue, sometimes you have to get it out of the way and break this rule. But if it's big and recurring, table that sucker until daytime when both of you are less tired and more generous with your affection. This one has saved us some major heartache.

4) This one is a little ridiculous, but it kinda works. If you're approaching DEFCON 4 (that point where you are gridlocked and all the loving energy has left the building), it's time for Cancer Mode. Super simple: Your significant other is dying of cancer. Not really, but imagine it. Seriously. Look them in the eyes, and before you launch your next shit-eating, passive-aggressive attack, imagine that they are on death's door and you won't get to be with them next week. If your imagination is halfway decent, this should provide an interesting context. The context could be as simple and terrifying as "You're dying? Good!" If that's the case, great! Get the divorce that is inevitable! If not (and in most cases, it is not the feeling you'll get) this awareness may soften your urge to win the argument at all costs. It may even contextualize how important you are to each other and how much you would miss the good things about them and your relationship if they were gone. And, not to be corny, but aren't we all going to die? Isn't our time with the ones we love limited anyway? This isn't a magic bullet, but it's a nice bit of context to consider.

5) This one may be the most important. And the hardest. It's called Fuck *Love Story*. If you remember, *Love Story* was a book published in 1970 that was made into an even more popular film due to its catchy tagline: "Love means never having to say you're sorry." We don't know what kind of world Erich Segal was living in, but in our world this is a very dangerous motto to live by. We would venture to say the exact opposite is true. Love, for us, means *always* having to say you're sorry. And we don't mean that you need to be a pushover for love to survive. We mean that love is deeply complex; love is about being generous, thoughtful, and humble. Love is about saying "I'm sorry," even if you desperately feel that you are one hundred percent right and have done nothing wrong. And the reason to say these words is because this is how the healing begins. This is the direct pathway back to the fun, goofy, loving energy that you both want back. And if you can somehow swallow your ego and muster these words, you are a goddamn hero. You are running into a burning building to save that last person even though you might die doing it. You are fighting the good fight, and that is what romantic love is all about.

AN APOLOGY, VERY LATE

Dear Daniel,

I cannot remember your last name. That in itself says way too much about the way I handled our living situation in 1995–1996.

In case you don't remember my last name, I am Mark Duplass. I was your freshman roommate at the University of Texas at Austin. Jester West dormitory. Fourteenth floor? Possibly. Can't remember. I had a soul patch and sideburns and a ridiculous haircut that consisted of long, curly locks that seemed to sprout forth from the back of my head like a mangled artichoke. I was in terrific physical shape, wore hemp necklaces, thrift store T-shirts, and an occasional pair of Tevas. I was upbeat and excited about my life. I listened to Dave Matthews Band on repeat and often preached the virtues of his lyrics: carpe diem, romance, positivity, and effervescence. I was, in short, an annoying, cocky eighteen-year-old kid who thought he had it all figured out. I could only see myself and my bright shining future. And I fear that, in this way and possibly a few more, I may have been insufferable to you.

But that is not what I want to apologize for. We were all idiots at eighteen years of age in some way or another, and I have forgiven myself for these mild atrocities. What I still struggle with today is how I treated you.

You were not like me. Yes, you had curly hair too. But that is where our similarities ended. You were the unhealthy kind of thin. Not athletic. You were shy. You seemed to be overwhelmed by the world and the changes we were all going through as college freshmen. I often found you alone in our shared dorm room, in the dark, lying on your bed, listening to PJ Harvey or the Red House Painters.

When I came in to that particular scene, I remember thinking, "Jesus, let's get some lights on and up this mood, yo!" And that is what I did. Turned on the jarring overhead fluorescent lights. Encouraged some different music. Offered one of my beers that I had stashed in the back of the mini fridge. And waxed philosophical about how awesome life was in an attempt to bring you up to my energy level.

What I did not do, not even once, was ask how you were doing. Or stop and listen to PJ Harvey's melancholic lyrics and realize that you may have been going through something similar. I never once offered to let you sit in the dark for a little bit longer so that you could move through whatever you were experiencing. Or, even better, give you some space and go somewhere else for an hour or so. I could only see my way of seeing the world . . . bright lights, Dave Matthews, forced positivity.

The funny thing is that the Red House Painters have become one of my favorite bands as I've gotten older. And I think about you a lot when I listen to them. Because I like to sit in the dark when I listen to them too. And I am often overwhelmed by the world and the very nostalgic melancholy that I assume you were feeling back in 1995.

So I first want to say thank you for introducing me to the

wonderful world of Mark Kozelek and the Red House Painters. I love the music. I am comfortable now in its sadness and don't feel the need to fight it anymore. More important, though, I want to say I'm sorry for not being a friend to you. For not even trying to understand you. For blasting weird, insensitive light into your dark, shy inner world. I get it now. But back then I simply did not understand it or make a legitimate attempt to understand it. I was a bit of a jam band hippie douchebag who was just trying to block out the darkness because I was, essentially, afraid of it. And for that, I am truly sorry.

Your freshman-year roommate,

Mark

TOP 10 FILMS OF ALL TIME (PART 3) *

And then there were twelve. And this is where it began to suck. We collectively agreed that all the films were representative of our taste. We also agreed that the films were empirically great and thus worthy of being included in the Top 10. We couldn't look to "the numbers" for a solution as we each had an equal amount of individual favorites and shared favorites at this point.

So we decided to play the game of inches. Instead of trying to get two films off the list, we would try to eliminate one. Each of us was tasked with picking the one he thought should go—and providing three reasonable arguments. Just like high school debate. But somehow (impossibly) dorkier.

We each spent an hour trying to convince the other of our respective choices. Neither of us budged.

Twelve movies. Ten slots. Two brothers. One list.

American Movie

Raising Arizona

Tootsie

Rocky

Hoop Dreams (JD)

The Crying Game

Dumb and Dumber

The Cruise

Henry Fool

The Horse Boy

You Can Count on Me

Close-Up (MD)

* *To be continued . . .*

YOU (AN EXERCISE IN EMPATHY)

PART I

FROM JOSH IN *The Puffy Chair* to John in *Cyrus* to Jeff in *Jeff, Who Lives at Home,* our stories' antiheroes are often called "lovable losers" by press and viewers. And this character archetype is one that both of us simultaneously love and resent. We truly love the unconventional protagonist's journey but resent that those characters are often reductively labeled as "losers" so that people can process them. Why can't they just be called people? That are sometimes lovable and sometimes not. Depending on who you are as a viewer. Depending on your mood that day. People whose lives you can experience and from whom you can learn a little something. Who make you feel a little differently. This approach to character is, in our opinion, storytelling at its best. Stories that don't clearly tell you what to feel about your protagonist. Stories that take you deep inside someone that you wouldn't normally look twice at on the street. Stories that, in short, simply put you in someone else's shoes for a bit so you can see the world through their strange, unexpected lens. . . .

You are a boy, almost a man. You are fifteen. You are wearing a blue denim jacket with a self-sewn Megadeth patch on the back. Your gray jeans are acid-washed, but not well, because you also did them yourself. Because your parents are poor. And you worked at your cousin's auto-body shop to save money for clothes and concerts for this summer. This is a summer you have been looking forward to for a long time. Because you hate school. Because you don't really fit in. And because the girls there don't like you. They call you Rat Face or sometimes Zit Face and also Pig.

But tonight this does not concern you as much as it normally does. Because tonight you have saved enough money to see your favorite new band. Your favorite new band is called Iron Maiden. It is 1980, and they have just released their first, self-titled record. The way it makes you feel when you listen to it is inexplicable. It is not separate from you. It is a part of you. The rare combination of death metal, prog rock, rock opera singing, and heartfelt lyrics . . . it's as if it were made for you. No, scratch that. It's as if *you* made it. Somehow. Through Iron Maiden. And it has come back to you, in thanks, to let you enjoy it. Tonight. Friday night. At the XYZ. A place that doesn't often ask for ID, thank God. Because you are only fifteen and have no legal business being inside this club, except for the fact that no one belongs here more than you.

But fuck all of this because here comes the band. Oh my God. You knew it. You just . . . you fucking knew it. Of course they would start with "Running Free." That drumbeat. You'd recognize it anywhere. One of the few drumbeats that you can play with minimal precision. Because you don't have enough money for drums and can only play on a makeshift set of empty paint cans you have assembled in your shared bedroom with your dipshit little sister, who is always ratting you out for bringing chocolate into your room. But, again, fuck all this. Because "Running Free" is in full swing now. . . .

I've got nowhere to call my own, hit the gas, and here I go.
I'm running free, yeah, I'm running free.

And you can't believe they sound better live than they do on the actual album but of course you can believe it because they are Iron FUCKING Maiden and this is the way they always were and always will be. And you know now more than ever that this is who you are, and this is where you belong, and that all these pretty girls around you who don't give a shit about you and look at those red marks on your face with disgust will never know the true beauty of you and Iron Maiden and how you are inextricably linked for all time. And you are confident that even though they smell delicious and that your raging boner *thinks* it is meant for them, it is not. Because they are not good enough for your boner. Your boner belongs with the gods tonight. And if it can't be with the gods, then, well, it can be with you and your hand back in your bedroom, after your stupid little sister goes to sleep and you get to have your boner and your chocolate and your memory of this perfect night with Iron Maiden, who, holy fuck, you still can't believe they sound this good live but of course you can believe it and—OH FUCK! Now they're gonna go right into "Phantom of the Opera"! The seven-minute prog opus that anchors the entire album. Of course they'd play it second . . . because when you have greatness like that in your back pocket you can't just sit on it, you have to let it REIGN!

And oh my God look at these girls nodding their heads. They probably don't even know this record. But they want Iron Maiden to think they do cuz maybe they can go backstage and . . . do whatever they would want to do with the band after the show. Like they're the real fans. And they're just dancing. And not even noticing that you can smell them and that they're actually rubbing against you, even though they were looking at you with those disgusted faces right before the show started and didn't want anything to do with you, now they're just "accidentally" rubbing up against you but you know deep down that you don't need them or want them even though they are so fucking hot and smell so good. . . . You know the eternal value of your boner and that you are smarter than your boner and you won't let it get excited about these dumb girls even though they smell so good and are so beautiful and the music is so incredible and it's almost like a perfect unexpected moment of God stuff and devil stuff that both weirdly seem so right to you right now—oh God, she just looked at me and smiled—oh God—oh FUUUUUUUUUCK!

Fuck.

Shit.

Really.

Come on.

And you know it. Immediately.

You know that you moaned out loud. And that even though she didn't hear you moan she could see you out of the corner of her eye. She could see you smiling and then closing your eyes in the existential gorgeous pain of you coming in your pants. She knew what happened.

Fuck.

And now it's like . . . different somehow. The music. It's different. You are different. She is different. She is somehow . . . more important. Bigger in the room. A force. Almost like . . . like *she* owns Iron Maiden now. Like, even though she doesn't even own the album or know any of the words, she stole your boner and she took Iron Maiden from your soul. And she's not gonna give it back. And it crushes you. And you fucking hate yourself for still being fifteen and for things like this making you cry and run out of the XYZ so no one can see you cry. And you ride your bike really fucking fast home and ignore the tears even though they might actually be freezing onto your cheeks in the bitter cold fast air coming at you. And you come right through the front door and you want to get to your room before your parents can ask "How was it?" but they catch you before you get there and ask the question and you gruffly say "Fine" and go to your (shared) room so your parents can't see you crying and your sister can't see you crying and you lie in your bed and you put your headphones on and you put on Iron Maiden's self-titled record in one last, desperate attempt to take it back from that shitty, vapid, hot, awesome-smelling girl who stole your boner and accidentally took Iron Maiden along with it. And you lie . . . and you lie . . . and you just lie . . . and you hope . . . and you hope . . . and you just hope . . . and you actually start to pray. Which you haven't done since you were five years old. And you pray that it will get easier. Somehow. Easier. And you don't believe it. But you pray. And you let "Prowler," the opening track, take you away.

VII.

AFTER THE FAILURE of our first feature film, *Vince Del Rio*, we had a hard time. We were still confused as to what went wrong with the film. We were now in our mid- and late twenties and the struggling-artist lifestyle was becoming less cute and more scary. All of our high school and college friends had found their footing and were experiencing varying degrees of success, all of which were astronomically greater than our own. That sucked. Even our parents, who were our strongest supporters, were beginning to plant the seeds of the "backup career" conversation.

As for us, we were still living in our crappy South Austin apartment, trying desperately to hold on to our dream before it drifted away. We spent half our days working at our editing business, which was barely enough to keep us afloat, and half our days taking walks, watching our favorite movies . . . searching endlessly for something that would help us "get there."

One day, as we were sitting in our typically depressed couch posture watching *Raising Arizona* for the thousandth time, Mark stood up, turned off the TV, and stared at me.

MARK: We are making a movie today.
JAY: About what?
MARK: I don't know.

(*Pause.*)

JAY: Uh . . . okay. I'm down for it, but . . .
MARK: But what?
JAY: We don't have a camera.
MARK: We still have Mom and Dad's.

> (*This was the camera we ultimately deemed unworthy to shoot even the behind-the-scenes footage for* Vince Del Rio *because it was so crappy.*)

JAY: But we don't have, like . . . a crew . . . or even a boom guy.
MARK: I don't care. We have to do something. Gimme $3. I'm going to 7-Eleven to get a mini-DV tape, and when I come back I want you to come up with a movie idea for us.

Mark, as usual, raced out before I could protest, not letting his own nerves and worries about the process show in front of me. He needed to project confidence to get us moving. This is part of our rhythm to this day.

I, on the other hand, was left holding the bag. A simultaneously annoying and empowering thing that Mark constantly does to me. He pushes me off cliffs and runs away, and I have to figure out the next move. I openly hate it and secretly love it because it shows how much Mark deeply believes in me. So I sat down and thought about what we might make. I banged my brain for an idea that didn't need much in terms of setting and production value. Maybe even something personal. Be-

fore long, an idea popped into my head. While in preproduction for *Vince Del Rio*, I had set up an answering service for the
film. While recording the outgoing greeting, I kept messing
up and rerecording it. It devolved into a bit of an existential
crisis for me by the fiftieth try, and something about the
whole process landed me in my bedroom crying that night.

Mark stormed back in with the tape and I greeted him with
this concept of recording an outgoing greeting, failing, and
having a semi–nervous breakdown in the process. Mark immediately lit up.

MARK: This is brilliant.
JAY: Great! Let's write the script.
MARK: Wait. I don't want to slow us down. We have momen-
tum. What if I just wing it?

(*Pause.*)

MARK: Like, you hold the camera and I'm gonna walk into that
kitchen and just . . . improvise it. Like we did with Brandt and
the Karate Master when we were kids. I'll try to record an answering machine greeting and fail at it. And you just film me.
And you can even talk to me during the take to throw ideas and
dialogue at me as we go. Like we used to do when we were little.
JAY: (*smiling*) Except this time you don't have to break your
shoulder holding the VTR.
MARK: (*smiling bigger*) Exactly.
JAY: Love it.
MARK: Love it.

I grabbed the camera bag and Mark went into our roommate Will's closet. Will was a computer programmer and had

some "grown-up" clothes (as we still call them, because we are children) for work. Mark grabbed a pair of black slacks and a green button-down. He came back into the kitchen to find me ready to go, with a few fun, readily available prop options I had grabbed. Some gas station sunglasses, a set of house keys, a cellphone, a bottle of wine, and, randomly, a small box of mints. Without saying anything more Mark positioned himself at the threshold of the kitchen. . . .

MARK: You rolling?
JAY: Yep.
MARK: Okay. I'm just gonna . . . just gonna come in and . . . see what happens?

As usual, Mark was good at leading the charge but got cold feet toward the end. And somehow whenever Mark got cold feet I was able to step in and push us that last few feet over the cliff. This is also part of our rhythm to this day.

JAY: Let's just have fun with it. No pressure.
MARK: Right.
JAY: Good luck. Love you.
MARK: Love you.

(*Heading out, stopping . . .*)

MARK: Wait. I need a character name.

(*This is Mark stalling because he is now fully scared. I think for a second and then reach for Mark's collar, reading the label.*)

JAY: Your shirt says "John Ashford" on it.

(*Pause.*)

MARK: It's perfect.

And with that, Mark went outside and came right back in. What happened next was one uninterrupted twenty-minute take of Mark trying and failing to get the answering machine greeting right. I moved around with the camera instinctually, zooming in and out as needed to get the right frame on the fly. I threw story and dialogue ideas at Mark along the way. Mark took them and ran with them. Taking sips of wine when it got difficult. Putting on the sunglasses when he got ashamed of his tenth failed attempt. Even sucking on a few of those random mints I gave him, as if he were trying to seduce the answering machine with his fresh minty breath. And then, a false emotional breakdown that suddenly became quite real for Mark due to all the stress we had been through with *Vince Del Rio* and the impending death of our lifelong artistic dream.

After the breakdown, while still filming, I leaned into the shot and whispered to Mark, "Now get up, and get the message right, but have it be as weird as possible." I didn't realize it at the time, but I was creating the dramatic structure of the film on the fly. As if all those hours spent watching HBO for the past fifteen years were paying off. I didn't even think about it. My internal movie barometer just knew what needed to happen. So Mark gathered himself and did it right then and there, without cutting.

After we had finished filming, we just sat and stared at

each other for a long while. We knew some kind of break-through had occurred. But we couldn't quite pinpoint it. We quickly called over our close friends and collaborators and showed them the take. We watched them watch it, and their faces said everything we were feeling. It was electric, raw, inspired, unpredictable. Somehow the energy of us not knowing where the story was headed could be felt in the footage. It was exciting for everyone. But it was also the crappiest-looking and -sounding footage we had ever shot. There was even a dead pixel in the center of the frame.

Over the next week, we tried to edit the footage down into something more cohesive, but we struggled getting the form right. Eventually we asked our friend David Zellner to take a look and see if he had any ideas. David had already had some success as a filmmaker, and we looked up to him and his brother, Nathan, as sources of inspiration. David loved the take and offered to edit it for us to see if he could crack something shorter and more like an actual film as opposed to just an inspired piece of footage.

Within a few days he handed us a ten-minute version, using jump cuts, that captured the spirit of what we shot but also gave it a more narrative pulse. Jay Deuby, our editing business partner, then weighed in. We all collaborated, and eventually we landed on a seven-minute final cut that we thought might be watchable as an actual short film. It needed a title, so we named it after the most prevalent piece of dialogue in a film about recording John's outgoing answering machine greeting: *This Is John.*

Now the film was done. But the problem was we had no idea what to do with it. Everyone who saw it really responded to it, but its extremely poor production value limited our avenues of exploitation. We thought about maybe just putting it on YouTube. Then we thought that maybe we should shelve it and try to make something similar but with better production value. Ultimately we decided to just pick one film festival and submit it to "see what happens." We chose (because we were idiots) Sundance. The most prominent and most difficult festival to gain entry to. We submitted it and quickly forgot about it.

In the meantime, we went back and revisited *Vince Del Rio,* and suddenly its failure and all the reasons for it were made abundantly clear to us. Yes, it was beautifully shot. Yes, the production value was amazing. But because we had unfortunately focused all of our energy on making a "professional" film, we had forgotten to focus on the most important elements . . . the performances and the story. And by accidentally stripping away all of those professional elements in our little answering machine movie (a full crew, proper set etiquette, trying to make the day on time and on budget) and instead focusing only on getting Mark's performance and the story right, we had stumbled onto something interesting. Perhaps even more important was the discovery of what *kinds* of topics we should be making films about. There's a saying that no one under the age of thirty makes a good film that's not autobiographical. And while that's not necessarily true, it proved to be helpful advice in our case. Why had we written a movie about a South Texas runner we knew nothing about, when our own personal foibles and way of seeing the world were what we happened to be in a unique position to offer? It took us a while to truly embrace the idea that the dramas of our relatively privileged middle-class life were film-worthy, but this moment was the beginning of that discovery.

A few months later, Mark was flying home to New Orleans

for Thanksgiving. My parents and I were waiting at the airport to pick him up. When Mark got off the plane, we greeted him with a homemade white poster-board sign that said "Filmmaker Registration." Mark just gave me a blank look.

JAY: Um . . . I just got a call. We got into Sundance.

(*Pause. Mark looks around for clues as to why I would say something like this. But he just sees more smiles from our parents.*)

MARK: This is not funny.
JAY: Mark . . . We. Are. In.

The four of us screamed and cried and jumped up and down in the Southwest terminal of the NOLA airport. And then we kept doing it.

THE BALL

WE'VE ALL SEEN it many times. It's the fourth quarter. The visiting team is driving down the field with under two minutes to go. They are down by one point. They go for it on fourth down for a second time on this drive. The chains come out. They barely get the first down. But the clock is still ticking. So the hurry-up offense kicks in, the coach saving that final time-out for when the team needs it most. They try a few passes. They don't work out. Then on third down they run the ball up the middle, landing on the opponent's thirty-four-yard line. Coach calls the final time-out with two seconds left to stop the clock. This final time-out with that much time left on the clock can only mean one thing . . . field goal.

Sure enough, the broadcast cuts to the sidelines and shows a rather smallish dude (at least by NFL standards) kicking a ball into a small net. Practicing before he is called onto the field to make or break the day with one last kick. And if you're anything like us, all you can think is "Dear God, I'm so glad I'm not him right now."

Because it's really unfair when you think about it. For sixty minutes, everyone else on the team has worked their asses off trying to claim victory. And now the team's destiny all comes down to this one guy who's been sitting on the sidelines for most of the game. This one guy who is infinitely smaller than everyone else on the team. This one guy who either makes the field goal or misses the field goal. Who wins or loses the game for the entire team. The pressure that he feels must be astronomical.

Growing up, we would watch these games on Sundays with our dad. All of us feeling so nervous for that poor kicker. And as we watched him prance out on the field, we were inevitably shocked at how calm he looked. How was that possible? It was a fun thing to talk about. You'd be surprised how often games play out like this. But one day our dad said something profound that we'll never forget. . . .

"At some point in your life you're going to be faced with this kind of situation. And almost every time you're going to be thinking, PLEASE DON'T GIVE ME THE BALL. I DON'T WANT THE BALL. IT'S TOO MUCH PRESSURE. And that's fine. It's how most people feel and it's how I've felt in most situations. But at some point, you're going to find yourself thinking, AS CRAZY AS THIS SOUNDS, I THINK I WANT THE BALL. I KNOW WHAT TO DO WITH IT. I'M UNIQUELY QUALIFIED TO HANDLE THIS SITUATION. SO . . . GIVE ME THE BALL. And when you find yourself feeling that way, you'll know you're in the right spot."

Of course, we are paraphrasing and making our dad sound a lot cooler and more prophetic than he really was, but that was the message and it has always stuck with us. We've felt that pressure onstage as musicians, as runners in high school, even as fathers, husbands, and brothers. And it has usually scared the shit out of us. But when it comes time to film a small, off-kilter story about people and how they relate to one another, we are always ready to step up and take the ball.

We want the ball because we truly feel that we are qualified to carry it. And we are also very thankful that, should we happen to drop the ball, none of our peers are three-hundred-and-fifty-pound linemen who can beat the ever-loving shit out of us.

PSYCHO

I STILL DON'T know why I did it. I was upset about something Jay did to me. But I can't remember what it was. Probably something small. But I had clearly decided to retaliate. With something big. So I waited patiently. For inspiration to come. Sitting quietly on the floor of the laundry room with revenge on my mind. I was seven. Jay was eleven.

Then I heard the upstairs shower turn on. And happened to notice a screwdriver with a translucent yellow handle next to the junk drawer. The same one Jay and I had bought our dad, together, for Father's Day. But as I stared at the screwdriver now, evil came to me. Which is kind of odd because I clearly loved this person. A lot. My sweet big brother. He taught me to read when I was only four years old. He included me in playtime with his friends when he didn't have to. But that screwdriver in my hand felt great. And something in me knew that I had to do something terrible with it.

So I marched up the seventeen shag-carpeted steps and down the hallway into our shared bathroom. I knew before I did what I did that, although Jay was a foot taller than me, he was standing in the sunken green tub and we would be eye to eye when the shit went down. I took a breath. I raised the screwdriver over my head. I gnarled my teeth. I loosened my throat in preparation for a guttural scream. And I reached for the shower curtain.

But then I stopped. I could see the immediate future. His terror. His potential retaliation against my retaliation. And I knew I couldn't follow through with it. I loved the guy. This was wrong. So I decided to just make a fun joke out of it. I lowered the screwdriver and casually opened the curtain with a faint "ha ha" and a loose, offhanded swipe of the screwdriver. I smiled, knowing he'd appreciate the smart humor. This would bridge our gap. This would solve whatever conflict we had at the moment. Less retaliation and more . . . reaching out.

What happened next is still a bit of a blur. But I do remember Jay's fragile, thin, hairless body slamming into the back of the shower, his face whiter than the subway tiles and his scream at a pitch level that, even though only half of its decibels were audible to the human ear, sent a lightning bolt up my spine and exploded my brain into stardust. I also remember seeing his emotions traveling quickly across his eyes. Fear, anger, and then (just before I turned and ran) hurt.

But I didn't stay for anything more. I took the seventeen stairs four or five at a time, past my terrified mother, out the front door, down the block, and all the way to the Lake Pontchartrain levee. And I hid myself in "the woods" (really just a ten-foot area of foliage between the levee and the lake, but it felt like an entire forest at age seven).

I'm not sure how long I stayed out there. If I had to guess I would say it was about twenty minutes. But a lot changed within me during that time. I was processing what had just happened. I was coming to the age of reason in my life. I was feeling something big that I couldn't put my finger on then but I now know was the innate desire for a young man to kill his God so he could be free. I remember feeling that I should not have done what I did to my awesome big brother but that I somehow needed to do it, and that I needed to stand by my actions and not apologize. Again, I couldn't understand this at the time, but I was just beginning my struggle with how to simultaneously be with and worship my God and still be an individual who could grow and breathe in this world on his own two feet.

And I remember deciding that when I got back home, I was not going to apologize. I was going to walk in and take my punishment like a man. Surely my parents would side with Jay. He had been harmed, and I was the clear offender. But something in me said, "Do not apologize for this. This is what you had to do."

So I marched back from the levee. I put my hand on the front door, steeling myself for the moment. And when I walked in, Jay was sitting on the couch, still undressed, hair wet, a towel wrapped around him like a boating accident survivor. My parents flanked him, arms around him, consoling him. He wasn't crying anymore, but his face had the ground-beef vibe of post-traumatic tears to it. And he just looked at me. And so did my parents. They were either unsure what to say or somehow knew that the bond between me and Jay was beyond them, that they had no right to interfere in what was about to happen. That it was our moment and had very little if anything to do with them.

And as I looked at Jay, something interesting happened. The desire I had to stand my ground and let him know that, while the incident may have been unfortunate, I was my own man and was capable of killing my God whenever I wanted . . . that desire was equally met by my desire to be next to him. More than that. To be *with* him in that moment. To be conjoined. A single unit. To come back to church and worship my God again so we could be that special duo that we'd always been. The Boys. And I was paralyzed with indecision as to how to be and what to say. And the funny thing is that he wasn't mad at me. He was just waiting to see what I would do. Patiently.

I think about that moment often. And whenever Jay does something that pisses me off or offends me, I think about how patient and loving he was to me then. How he let me do that to him without retaliation, somehow sensing that I needed to figure out where I stood with him. It plays like an eternal IOU in our relationship. And I try my best to let whatever is bothering me slide. Sometimes it works.

VIII.

We flew to Sundance in 2003 with a thousand postcards, a thousand business cards, and a thousand DVD copies of our crappy-looking $3 short film, *This Is John*, to hand out for free to any industry person we met. We were vastly overprepared for the world to receive us and lavish upon us praise, opportunity, and fortune. As you might imagine, things did not go down quite like this.

What did happen was that we were made aware of all the very cool parties at Sundance to which the short-film makers were *not* invited. So we spent a good portion of our early days there feeling bad about being snubbed, becoming obsessed with what was actually going on inside of those parties, and then concocting schemes by which to gain entrance into said parties. The lamest of which, I believe, was Mark realizing that David Arquette had a film at the festival, that I looked somewhat like David, and that we could try to gain entrance to the parties by pretending I was David Arquette. This seemed like our best option, until we realized that neither of us had the balls to try this tactic and risk the grand embarrassment of being rejected in wide view of everyone on Main Street. Not to mention WHAT IF DAVID ARQUETTE WAS ALREADY AT THE FUCKING PARTY?

So instead we went back to our "just out of town" (way out of town) ski lodge and watched a bunch of eighties movies on VHS. If memory serves, *SpaceCamp* held up pretty well.

However, once our little short film started to screen, something very interesting happened. Despite being the ugliest and worst-sounding film in the festival's history, we became a bit of a cult hit. There was a lore to our little movie . . . a "Look what these guys did with only $3" kinda thing. And industry people started to seek us out. Being underdogs seemed to serve us, and this was a status we would soon learn to embrace.

By the end of the festival, a fair amount of industry folks knew who we were, and we were asked to fly to Los Angeles to meet with a top-tier agent at William Morris (one of the big four agencies at the time). He signed us on the spot and we realized we had made it!

But not really. Because that agent simply asked us to "write a feature script you want to make and I'll help you package it." We didn't know what that meant, so we asked around and it turned out that "packaging" sounded really cool. It means that the agent takes your script and seeks out famous actors who are also represented by that agency to "attach" to your movie, then goes out and gets financing to make the movie. Simple. Easy.

But not really. Because the more we talked to peers who were a few steps ahead of us in this whole independent film game, the more we realized that packaging is a lot like the Waiting Place in *Oh, the Places You'll Go!* Filmmakers often sit there for years, feeling *so close* to getting their movie made but never quite getting there. Or perhaps even worse, getting so desperate after a few years of waiting that they take what-

ever cast and financier they can get and end up making a bas-
tardized version of their passion project.

We didn't want to end up in the Waiting Place, and we already had a failed feature film under our belt with *Vince Del
Rio*. So we decided to make another short and slowly increase
the scope of our work. Keep it safe and comfortable but try to
grow a little bit. This next short would have (wait for it) . . .
two actors instead of one. It would still be made for under
$100 in a few hours. And it would also take place in a kitchen.
We added Katie Aselton (Mark's then-girlfriend) as an actor
opposite Mark, and we got a real boom operator to get decent
sound (John Robinette, the drummer from Mark's band, Volcano, I'm Still Excited!!). We also bought a $3,000 twenty-
four-frame DV camera and rented it out to pay it off.

The new short was called *Scrapple* (actually, we initially
called it *Scrabble*, but a large company quickly let us know this
name was spoken for . . . so we quickly changed the title). The
film was about a couple who fights over a board game as the
truth about their failing relationship comes spilling out. This
also went to Sundance (in 2004) and did very well at the festival. By now our agents were beating down our doors for a
good feature script to package, so we started to discuss what
kind of feature we would want to make . . . how to draw upon
the success of *This Is John* and *Scrapple* and avoid the pitfalls of
Vince Del Rio.

The first one we came up with failed spectacularly at both
sets of criteria. It was a surrealist black comedy thriller called
Unlimited Night and Weekend Minutes. It picked up right where
This Is John left off, except after the cut to black . . . a gunshot
was heard! And John Ashford woke up on a desolate island.
Uncertain whether he was in the afterlife, an alternate uni-

verse, or a dream, John explored the island for signs of life. He met a love interest, a Mr. Miyagi–esque mentor, and a villainous monster-man hybrid named Bik, and somehow remained in contact with an agoraphobic Verizon Wireless representative (via his cellphone), who ultimately helped John Ashford transcend his fears and become the hero he always hoped he would be.

We wrote a draft of this, sent it to our agent, who very politely (his voice filled with tons of regret for ever signing us) let us know that this was an "unpackageable" film and that we should try something else. This was a bummer, but we understood, and then submitted the second script we were working on, which was called, unbelievably, *Boobs in the Night*. Written for Paul Giamatti to star (he still doesn't know this—hi, Paul!), it was a comedic drama set in the world of Girls Gone Wild and followed an ex–porn addict who tries to exact revenge on the people who beat him up while on spring break. This movie was also "not quite right" for our agent to package and we began to get the sense that maybe we weren't as Hollywood as we thought.

Soon we realized that the only way we were going to keep moving forward was to keep making films ourselves. We learned from Linklater and Rodriguez in Austin that you could make a truly cheap feature on your own, so we set about trying to write something that was doable on a micro-budget. Having blown our previous savings on *Vince Del Rio*, we asked our parents whether they would stake us a $10,000 loan to make this feature if we could write one that was worthy. As always, they were incredibly supportive and agreed to lend us the money.

Now all we had to do was come up with the movie.

From: mark duplass
To: jay duplass
Subject:

do u ever feel like u have to act different with me when there are other people around?

_____

From: jay duplass
To: mark duplass
Subject: RE:

kinda. do u feel like it's just me that does it?

_____

From: mark duplass
To: jay duplass
Subject: RE:

NO! sorry. didn't mean it to come across as an accusation. ha. email sucks. what I meant was I feel like we both do it.

it's been bothering me lately and I don't know why it's happening. glad to hear that u also feel it. wanna get into it?

———————————

From: jay duplass
To: mark duplass
Subject: RE:

fo sho. u start?

———————————

From: mark duplass
To: jay duplass
Subject: RE:

for me it bothers me bc I feel most comfortable around you
when it's just the two of us. and then the energy totally shifts
when someone else comes into the room. it's like I have to
change our dynamic to open up the world to fit everyone else
in it or something. does that resonate at all with u?

———————————

From: jay duplass
To: mark duplass
Subject: RE:

100%. it's like we're in the middle of telling each other a
story that u and I both know intimately, and then we have to
go all the way back to the beginning and tell everyone else
the "setup" to get people on board. which works for them,

but leaves u and me in the weird spot of hearing part of the story we've already heard 1,000 times.

———————

From: mark duplass
To: jay duplass
Subject: RE:

yes! and even worse is that we have to pretend like we're hearing it for the first time so that we can get along with the new people in the room. it's really kinda fucked up. and I don't know how to get around it.

———————

From: jay duplass
To: mark duplass
Subject: RE:

me neither. but I'm glad u r bringing this up. I did something really fucked up the other day that I wasn't gonna admit but now feel like maybe I can. don't get mad. but at the big "night before" party I actually saw you across the room. I was in the middle of a good conversation with someone I had just met and I was in that party mode where I wanted to meet new people (which is rare for me). And I deliberately didn't go over and say hi to you. And I didn't really understand why I did it and it kinda bothered me. But now I'm realizing it was probably because I was in the mode to hang with and meet new people and that's just kinda hard to do sometimes if you and I are in our weird little internal brother mode.

———————

From: mark duplass
To: jay duplass
Subject: RE:

ha! I love that u ducked me at a party. not mad. totally get it. that's part and parcel with this other part of it for me . . . sometimes I have a hard time being with u at a party bc we are so similar in our "social voices"? like we have the same jokes and party stories and similar party energy and I feel like when we're both doing it at the same time it feels odd. like, if you're feeling particularly "on" I just kinda sit back and let u do it. or vice versa.

———————————

From: jay duplass
To: mark duplass
Subject: RE:

totally. side note: does anyone else have these conversations? are we weird?

———————————

From: mark duplass
To: jay duplass
Subject: RE:

I think we might be weird. But I kinda don't care.

———————————

From: jay duplass
To: mark duplass
Subject: RE:

me neither. so, any solutions come to mind?

———————

From: mark duplass
To: jay duplass
Subject: RE:

I guess maybe we give each other permission to duck each other every now and then at a party and to also allow ourselves to feel weird and not worry about it too much when we try to enmesh with other people?

———————

From: jay duplass
To: mark duplass
Subject: RE:

I'm down. kinda makes us sound super unhealthy and codependent. which is probably true. oh well.

love u,

peepee johnson the elder

IX.

Looking back at that time after we made our first two Sundance shorts and were writing the insane failed scripts that were *Unlimited Night and Weekend Minutes* and *Boobs in the Night,* it's clear to us now what we were trying to do. Even though our first two short films were personal, small stories based on elements of our own lives, we still did not trust or believe in our hearts that those stories were "film-worthy." Thus the ridiculous, ostentatious plotting of the two above-mentioned feature scripts. Luckily, it only took us two wasted attempts to figure this out, and we were able to refocus on what was working for us . . . drawing from our lives and the specific sense of humor and sadness we felt in the world. Today we call this mining the "epically small" elements of our lives. Back then, though, we were still scared and floundering . . . just trying to make a feature film that didn't suck.

After our parents generously agreed to lend us the $10,000 cost for a new feature film, Jay and I realized that we had everything we needed to start production. We owned our camera outright (we had rented it out enough to pay it off). We had a good boom microphone (which we had also rented out to pay off). And we had a system for the rest of the gear that was ethically questionable (but highly functional) where we would buy work lights and extension cords from a certain big-box hardware store and return them before thirty days for our money back. So basically we were set. Good to go. Time to make a movie.

And this is where things got tricky. As artists and entrepreneurs, we often spend a lot of our time dreaming of what we could do if only we had the money, the connections, and the opportunities. This is often just a defense mechanism to cover up the fact that we may, deep down, just not be good enough. And when you are suddenly faced with the fact that you have all the practical tools you need to make your dreams come true, it can often be a crippling and humbling experience. Thus we found ourselves fully equipped to make our feature, but story inspiration was not coming.

So we did what we had learned to do when things got hard and confusing. We took walks. And an interesting thing happened. Every time we scheduled a "creative session" to work on our movie, one of us ended up preempting the creative talk because we were having some sort of relationship troubles that needed discussing. It became a joke after a while. And not just for us. Among our friends (we were all in our mid- to late twenties at the time) it seemed everyone was in some sort of relationship that was on the precipice of growing or dying. The big question everyone was facing was essentially "We've been dating for a while now. It seems we need to shit or get off the pot. Are we planning to go the distance? And if not, shouldn't we just break up and not waste any more of our good years on something that isn't going to last?"

And the more we thought about this, the more we felt that this whole area should serve as the subject matter for our new movie. It was what we knew, and we were in a unique position to be an authority on this topic. We would place a young couple at the center of our movie who was dealing with this very issue . . . and *that* would be our central story. We wanted it to have the raw, emotional truth of a John Cassavetes film but also carry our sense of goofiness and humor. We didn't want people to have to eat their vegetables with this one. Or at least if they were vegetables, they would be roasted with lots of salt and olive oil and be super crispy and fun! (Can't believe we just wrote that, but you get it.)

We then set about the casting. Yes. We know. We didn't have characters or a script yet, so how could we cast? Well, our idea was to decide who would be *in* the film first. Find people we liked, who we knew were talented, easygoing, and fun to be with . . . and then write the roles specifically for those people. In this way, we could tailor the parts to avoid their weaknesses and focus on their strengths. We knew Jay would hold the camera and I would be in it, as that process had worked well in our previous two short films, and having one of the filmmakers acting inside the scenes to guide any improvisations was extremely helpful. We also knew Katie was the best actress in our orbit and that she and I had good onscreen chemistry (based on our short film *Scrapple*), so she was the next one pinned down. Then Jay had the idea that we should include a third person, so it wasn't *all* just relationship talk. Someone inherently funny but not in an "I'm trying to be funny" way. Someone whose personal style would greatly contrast with mine and provide humor and counterpoint by the sheer difference in personality. Jay had worked with Rhett Wilkins in an acting class in Austin, and he was the perfect fit. His dreamy, relaxed energy would be a great combat zone for the more type-A alpha vibe I planned for the character of Josh.

Once we had our main cast, we set about discussing the plot. Like with the casting process, we approached this one a bit backward. We started to develop our "available materials" school of filmmaking without knowing it. By this we mean we looked at our lives and asked ourselves, "What do we own or have access to that we can use in the film for free?" We were all living in Brooklyn at the time, just a few miles from one another, so we began meeting at my apartment to discuss. A few obvious things jumped out at us:

1) DUH, MARK'S APARTMENT

This was a 750-square-foot place Mark rented along with three other guys. But they were all artists and close friends and would happily vacate whenever needed so we could shoot in there. Done.

2) KATIE'S APARTMENT

Likewise, Katie lived with our friend and fellow sympathetic artist Maggie Phillips (who would become our music supervisor on this film and almost every other project of ours in the future), and she was sensitive to the cause. Location #2, done.

3) MARK'S VAN

This ended up being a *big* deal. Not only was it a cool set piece, it was functional in that we could transport the entire cast and crew in the van. And it would act as the picture vehicle in the movie as well. And be our equipment truck. Three for one! Done.

4) THE TOWN OF MILBRIDGE, MAINE

Katie is from a small blue-collar fishing village in
Maine of less than a thousand people. Her father, Carl,
is the black-bag doctor everyone loves. We realized that
trying to shoot exteriors anywhere near Manhattan
would be a nightmare, but shooting in a small town
where everyone loves Katie and would be actually interested in supporting a movie (instead of being annoyed by us) would be extremely helpful. Plus, we
could all crash in Katie's parents' basement for free. So,
the town of Milbridge, Maine. Done.

Once we realized we would shoot in Milbridge, we took a
trip up there in the van and scouted all the cool-looking
places we could shoot that were friendly to our cause. These
included the local clam shack, an odd used-furniture depot
next to an auto shop just outside of town, the local motel and
restaurant, and Carl's best friend Ozzie's woodsy camp about
thirty minutes away.

All of these elements went into the creative pot, and from
there we started building the story. The town of Milbridge
was generic-looking enough that we felt we could double it
for multiple towns, so we decided on a road movie. A road
movie where the central relationship would be tested and we
would raise and ultimately answer the simple question "Is
this couple going to get married, or will they break up?" Simple. Relevant to our generation. And something we were au-
thorities on due to it being an epidemic among our current
group of friends (including ourselves). The only thing we
were missing was that fun, goofy element that would make

the film different from your average eat-your-vegetables relationship drama that had been done so many times before.
So we started discussing things that are just inherently funny.
Or silly. And we remembered how obsessed with recliners
our grandfather was when we were little. How big and im-
practical they were. How situated in a certain place in American history they were (at least for us). And how road movies
usually have some sort of quest. A holy grail of sorts. When we
started talking about this stupid recliner being the ultimate
quest of the road trip, the movie started to feel very "us."

From here, the script came relatively quickly to us and we
felt good about what we had. We sent it to our agent, letting
him know that we planned to make it ourselves. Oddly
enough, he actually loved it and asked to "package" it for us.
He felt it was something we could get a few movie stars in (not
me, Katie, or Rhett) and get a few million dollars to do and
then sell at Sundance (not unlike the model of Zach Braff's
Garden State, which had been so successful the previous year).
He pledged his undying support, and for a moment we considered it. Why not let this powerful agent take our tiny movie
up a few notches? Why not get paid to do it instead of borrowing money from our parents that we might never be able to
pay back? It was tempting. But the horror stories of waiting
years at the packaging bus stop weren't enticing. We also believed in me, Katie, and Rhett as the leads and didn't want to
recast. And knowing that we had the tools we needed to make
it our way and be able to control it creatively and practically
from top to bottom was too good to pass up.

So we turned down our agent's generous request (we could
hear his jaw hit the floor on the other end of the line) and
decided to make the movie on our own. We assembled a bare-
bones cast and crew in addition to me, Jay, Katie, and Rhett.

We added our third unofficial brother, Jay Deuby, as editor and our good friend and filmmaker John Bryant from Austin as an all-around utility player (hanging lights and holding the boom mic, among many other things). We would all work for free. We set a production date of summer 2004, which would give us enough time to edit and submit it for Sundance 2005, where we hoped to sell the film, then pay back our parents and share the profits among our six-person wrecking crew.

The film would be called *The Lazy Boy*. Which we soon realized was not only a stupid title, it was also a bad pun. So we decided to simplify it. Make it a touch goofier. Like the movie itself. We eventually settled on *The Puffy Chair*.

LEMONS

Hi there. It's me, Mark. I'm alone. Jay is currently on set for *Transparent*. He has a cough. He is tired and overworked. So here is a good example of the many benefits of being in a partnership like the one we have. We do a lot of divide-and-conquering. It's partially how we stay so prolific. Sometimes we even lie and say something is being done by both of us when really only one of us is doing it and the other is checking it to make sure it doesn't suck. And the work rarely suffers. Anyhow, it's just me on this one. Hope that's cool. I'm actually kind of psyched. I have a story to tell that is personal and ultimately easier to tell on my own.

I have been a very intense person my whole life. For example, from the moment I picked up the drums at age ten, I practiced for hours every day. Same for the guitar at thirteen. I played my cheapie acoustic monster with my prepubescent hands until they cramped and bled. I have always been of the opinion that if you want to make it as an artist, you better be willing to sacrifice almost everything to get there (more on this very dangerous way of thinking later). So I played hard, and for long hours, and by the time I was sixteen I was playing singer-songwriter gigs around New Orleans, and by the time

I was twenty-one I found myself on a U.S. tour for four months with my first CD for sale out of the back of my purple conversion van.

I moved to New York City to further my music career and eventually started a band that signed a good record deal and kept me on the road a bunch, while simultaneously working with Jay to build our film career. It was an intense time, I was overworking myself as usual, and just as my film and music careers were taking off I started getting pains in my hands, arms, and neck. It progressed quickly, and soon my upper body had pretty much crapped out and failed me. After years of abuse of my hands and arms, my torso had all but shut down—inflammation and repetitive stress injuries so bad it hurt to open a door, much less play guitar. I couldn't even sit at my computer for longer than ten minutes without cramping up in physical pain.

This was not only physically challenging, it was an emotional struggle as well, because at the time the most important thing I was supposed to be doing was . . . yep, sitting at my computer and writing *The Puffy Chair*. After having had two shorts at Sundance, this was the next step. The world was waiting, so was Jay, and I was basically crippled.

And that's when the depression set in. I was furious with myself for pushing my body so hard, and I was angry at the world for giving me an opportunity to make movies and then shutting the door in my face by taking away my ability to physically write.

So I pouted a whole bunch. Jay offered to step up and take over the writing, but at that time we had much more of an early Coen Brothers division of labor, where I was leading the writing and producing and he was leading the directing.

My now-wife, Katie, was amazing. Though we were still in the early years of dating at the time, she stuck with me like a dutiful long-term spouse. She would come to my house for "writer sessions" where I would talk out script ideas with her and she would type them into the computer for me. It was an incredibly sweet and selfless move on her part, but I was fussy and the process ultimately was too verbal and intellectual to truly tap into the kind of writing I wanted to do.

So I pouted some more. And sank into a deeper depression. I felt trapped and could only think about how wronged I was and what my new physical limitations were keeping me from accomplishing. How there was only one way to write (me at my computer pounding it out) and how since I couldn't perform in that way, I was done.

Feeling utterly lost, I started taking long, rambling walks trying to think about other things I could do. Even other careers. I mused about all kinds of things that didn't require intense usage of my hands and arms.

And then something odd happened. I had a flash from my past. I remembered in the eighties when my dad, who was a trial attorney in New Orleans, would pace back and forth in our living room with his big Dictaphone held to his mouth, working out his opening arguments. Recording. Pausing. Talking. Thinking. I remembered how he looked while he was birthing the ideas. It was the same way I used to feel when I was writing a song or writing short films at my computer. The ideas were flowing and he could just spit them right out as they came.

I turned around and headed for the RadioShack on Manhattan Avenue in Brooklyn. I bought a $20 handheld cassette recorder that looked a lot like my dad's Dictaphone. I bought three tapes and batteries. Then I went to the grocery store and bought a hundred index cards, a black Sharpie, and a pack of shitty blue Bic pens. I was running now.

Back at my apartment I ripped open the index cards and started writing down the names of scenes with the black Sharpie:

JOSH AND EMILY INTRO

PICKING UP THE CHAIR

THE BIG MOTEL FIGHT

Then I would flip them over and write brief descriptions of what should happen in the scenes.

Over the next few days, Jay and I cobbled together on those notecards what we thought would make up the basic scene structure for *The Puffy Chair*. It was a stack of about twenty scenes and their brief descriptions on the back. I cleared my calendar for a few days and locked myself in my room with the stack of cards. I lit a shitty candle and got some tea and lay down in my bed, a work scenario where my arms gave me no pain. And I took my Dictaphone, pressed record, and just started talking. . . .

"Josh, Emily, and Rhett meet a sketchy guy at a furniture warehouse and discover the chair is not as advertised. . . ."

When it came time for writing dialogue I would just say:

"Josh, colon, YOU'RE TELLING ME THAT CHAIR IS THIS CHAIR?"

"Emily, colon, JOSH, LET'S JUST GO."

I felt pretty stupid at first, but something kind of amazing happened. Because I couldn't see what I was writing, I just kept going. I didn't have the chance to look at what I had just written and criticize it like I used to do on my computer. It was a linear, unstoppable process, and it just put me on a river of story and dialogue and I floated down it.

I would press pause here and there to catch my breath and find a new thought, and I would occasionally even cheat, rewind, and rerecord a bit of dialogue if I knew instantly I could improve it, but overall it was a straight shot getting that first scene done.

Katie was nice enough to transcribe it, cleaning up my grammatical errors and tightening some of the verbose prose in the process. I brought it to Jay, and when he read it he had the exact reaction I had. It was clumsily written and not very eloquent in its scene descriptions, but the dialogue felt very natural, and the pacing was nearly impeccable. Somehow, speaking and performing the script live had made my writing better than it had ever been.

Jay ran the scene through Final Draft's screenwriting software and used his powers of precision (our faithful closer) to make it better and sharper, while I barfed out the next scene into my shitty Dictaphone. We continued this process the next day . . . me the barfer, Jay the cleaner and refiner. Within two weeks we had the first draft of *The Puffy Chair,* and it was hands down the best script we had ever written.

I took a long walk to Katie's apartment the night we finished. I was twenty-six and I remember thinking that anything was possible. That the worst thing that had ever happened to me in my life had led me to a writing process that made me a better writer than I ever hoped to be.

I was being highly dramatic, but I felt so good I didn't care. I just kept saying, over and over, "Lemons. Lemonade."

Pretty sure Beyoncé stole that from me. But it's cool.

HIKES

FOR THOSE OF you who are thinking, "I wish my sibling and I got along like Mark and Jay," please know that being as inextricably intertwined as we are has its sizable downsides. And we constantly struggle to find the right ways to deal with the issues that arise from our extreme closeness. One of the major problems is that we love each other very much and we're both criers, so that when it comes time to talk about these things we often either can't get through the conversation without breaking down or, once we see that we are putting the other one in pain, backing away from the conflict and leaving the issue unresolved. This is where hiking comes into play.

We discovered by accident one day that hikes are a great way to hammer out our big issues. First off, they offer a wide-open space, so our fear of being publicly humiliated helps somewhat to keep the waterworks at bay. More important, when one is hiking one has to constantly look forward so that one does not fall and break a limb or a crucial part of one's face. This is a good problem for us in this particular situation. It means that we must look down at the terrain and thus we don't have to look at each other while we are airing our grievances.

A few years ago we went through a particularly hard time. There has always been a discrepancy in our work appetites. In particular, I like to fill my work plate with way too much food, while Jay tends to be choosier and only pick the things he knows he wants to eat. This conflict is one we are no strangers to and have a good deal of experience with, but it became a little more complex as my acting career outside of our own filmmaking began to take off. Being on FX's *The League* and having to adhere to its shooting schedule was proving at times to be an obstacle to making our own films. Often that meant Jay would have to pick up my slack or (even worse) that we couldn't actually shoot one of our projects because I had a contractual acting obligation elsewhere. Fearing that Jay was upset, I would politely check in and make sure he was okay with things. Jay was always generous and understanding, but he's also a human being. A bit of resentment began to build up.

Then a film-directing project fell into our laps that was exciting to both of us. It felt like this could be the follow-up film to our second studio movie, *Jeff, Who Lives at Home,* that we were looking for. The problem was that our HBO show, *Togetherness,* was on the horizon, and I also had another season of *The League* to act in before it started. Long story short, Jay had a small window in which to make this film before *Togetherness* started for both of us, but I was simply not available during that window. Our credo had always been that we would write and direct films together or we wouldn't do them at all. And that credo kept us and our brand healthy for a long time. In fact, that solidarity is the main reason we are standing where we stand today as filmmakers. We both truly believe that we would never be where we are without having stuck together the way we did in our formative years. In this case, however, we were both passionate about the film, but only one of us was available to direct it.

I was bummed but not worried. I assumed that Jay would be fine to let this movie go. After all, our credo was our credo. Jay, however, was not ready to let this one go and assumed I would understand opening the conversation to his directing this movie by himself.

The subject came up naturally during a writing session in our office for our first season of *Togetherness*. Jay, being forever sensitive but also opportunistic enough to seize an opening when he saw one, lightly floated the idea of what it would feel like if "one day we directed a few episodes of *Togetherness* individually and not as a team. Like, down-the-line kinda thing." I was open to the idea. After all, we had co-branded the show, we co-produced it, we co-wrote the episodes. Could be fun in, say, season three or four to try one on our own. So, a small brick having been paved on the way to his main agenda, Jay then ever so gently floated the idea of taking on directing this new movie by himself while I was shooting *The League*.

This did not go well.

In a rare moment where emotion took over our delicate sensitivity and care for each other, I became extremely offended and, somewhat irrationally, asked Jay if he had secretly been just wanting to go out on his own and direct by himself all along. Jay, of course, denied it and said it was just about the timing. I then took a nasty step forward and essentially accused Jay of wanting to get out of our partnership but not being willing to own up to it. Jay became defensive and upset that I was projecting my feelings onto him. It was all shaping up to be a rather juicy episode of *Real Housewives*. Before it went further, I decided to go home and sleep it off.

This was the only time in our lives where we went more

than a day without speaking because of an argument. Jay was upset and bewildered at the extreme level of hurt I was experiencing, and I was feeling deeply rejected and afraid that he secretly wanted to start making films without me. Finally, I calmed down enough to call Jay and ask him to go for a hike. In particular, a hike with some rather rigorous terrain that would provide sufficient excuse to avoid each other's eyeballs as we tried to work through this one. Jay accepted.

When we began the hike, it took a little while to get into it. It felt like a seminal moment in our relationship. And neither of us was quite sure where this conversation would take us. Our memory of it is something like this. . . .

JAY: Look, I just want to say that I'm sorry this has been so hurtful to you.
MARK: Thanks for saying that. I appreciate it.
JAY: And I don't want to diminish in any way what you're feeling, but I have to say that I just don't fully understand the depth of your hurt on this one.
MARK: I know, I know. I think I didn't fully understand it either. But the more I sat with it, the more I realized that I was just afraid that you wanting to do this movie on your own was less about the timing of it and more reflective of, like . . . you maybe wanting to do more stuff on your own. Without me.

(*Jay nods. Mark waits.*)

JAY: Well, I can assure you that this never would have come up if you were available. I would have totally proceeded with us doing this together like normal.
MARK: Okay.

JAY: Okay?

MARK: Okay.

(At this point I make the mistake of looking up at Jay and realizing that as much as we both want to believe what Jay is saying is true, it just isn't one hundred percent true.)

MARK: But the weird part is that we could have talked about directing this next year together. But the first place you jumped to was doing it when I wasn't available . . . without me.

JAY: Well, I guess I was just assuming we'd do another season of *Togetherness* next year. You'd do another season of *The League*. There would be no time for you to direct a movie then either. And it would go away.

MARK: But we don't know that for sure. You're just assuming that.

JAY: Because it's the most likely scenario.

MARK: But you didn't even entertain pushing it to a time frame when we could do it together?

JAY: Okay. I hear you. I mean, I thought about it. I guess I just didn't verbalize it to you. . . .

(At this point we both realize we are getting defensive again, and we slow down the talking and walking.)

MARK: Hey. Look. I know it's not always the easiest process in the world working together. I know I kind of bully you into things sometimes. And my brain doesn't work like yours and . . . like . . . it can be hard. I guess I'm saying . . . while it would totally suck, if you felt like you wanted a little freedom and space and that you might actually *prefer* to do this one on your own, then you need to tell me. It's okay.

(*Jay takes a bit of time with this one. And before he opens his mouth, I already know the answer. And it almost kills me.*)

JAY: I mean. I'm sorry. But . . . yeah. There's a part of me that's bummed that you get to go off and act in other people's projects and I have to wait for you to be available.

MARK: Totally. I totally get it.

JAY: And I'd be lying if I didn't say it was . . . interesting to me to think about doing something on my own. At my own speed. The way I wanna do things.

MARK: I get that too.

JAY: You do?

MARK: Yes! I guess it's easier for me because I've had all this creative experience as an actor outside of our little brother union and you really haven't had any.

JAY: Exactly.

MARK: And honestly? It's *really* fun. I love being the only one in the room with our specific skill set and energy. I get all the praise!

(*We laugh about this and start walking again, the tension lifting a little bit.*)

MARK: And I also get to be whoever I want to be when you're not around.

JAY: It's weird you said that. Because as much as I love what we have, it's like we know each other so well that when I'm around you I don't get to flex weird new sides of myself. Because you know me well. And it would feel false in front of you.

MARK: Totally get it. On the set of *Humpday* I got to smoke weed and talk about different stuff and be a little different. And there was no one there who knew me inside and out to call me on my bullshit.

(This is really funny to us for some reason.)

JAY: And to be super clear, this wouldn't mean I don't want to direct with you anymore, just so you know. I'm not even sure I definitely want to do this on my own.

MARK: No. I understand. I think maybe those old rules of us being a tightly knit brand that only writes and directs together might be a little . . .

JAY: Constrictive or something.

MARK: Maybe.

(We get quiet. The joy of laughing is over, and we are centered again on the gravity of this decision and what it will mean for us as business partners and brothers.)

JAY: How are you feeling?

MARK: Um . . . I am scared that you are gonna realize that you might enjoy making movies on your own better than when you make them with me . . . and that will be the beginning of the end of what we have.

JAY: I don't think that's gonna happen.

MARK: I'm still scared. But I love you and I want you to be happy. And if this is something you need to pursue I think you should do it.

Jay: Really?

Mark: No. Not really. But yes. Really.

Jay: I love you. Thanks for being so open. And I'm sorry it hurt.

Mark: I'm sorry I was so overly sensitive. I love you too.

(This is the crying part. You don't need to see this.)

As we walked back to the car, we switched the conversation to something easier. I can't remember what it was about, but it definitely allowed us to analyze something outside of ourselves. Maybe even allowed us to be a little superficial and catty about something or someone. A chat that clearly placed the two of us together against the world, so we could feel that comfort of being fully aligned with each other like we were when we were little, together in the same twin bed.

UNSOLICITED ADVICE PART 2
CARS

THIS ONE IS really simple.

BUY THE KIA!
OR THE HYUNDAI!!

Or whatever the version of this car is whenever you read this stupid chapter.

Because these cars are extremely well made.

They are the cheapest on the market.

They come with 100,000-mile and ten-year warranties (as opposed to many others that are less than half that amount).

Anything more than this is vanity.

Save your money for a rainy day.

Moving on!

This message is brought to you by Nick Kroll.

THE CAVALRY ISN'T COMING

WHEN WE GO to film festivals and meet aspiring filmmakers, we get one question more than any other:

"How do you make it in this brutal fucking business?"

Some use much worse language. While we have no definitive answer for this question, we remember all too well that feeling of "I am inspired and full of weird magic and I feel like I'm probably going to die before I get a chance to share it with the world because no one can hear me." And we get it. That's how we felt. It's where we came from. So, not to get all Tony Robbins up in here, but we are going to get a little bit Tony Robbins and guide you through a process of how to get somewhere when you're coming from nowhere. Again, it's not the only way to get there. It's just reflective of the way *we* got there, and frankly it's the only way we know how to do it. The good news is you don't need connections or nepotism with this path . . . you just need to be desperately driven, hardworking, and honest with yourself. And while this example pertains to filmmaking, we suppose you could extrapolate it to other fields (except maybe professional curling). It begins with a simple acknowledgment:

THE CAVALRY ISN'T COMING.

If we were Tony Robbins, we'd call it a catchphrase. Even look you in the eyes with a serial killer's all-knowing intent and repeat it. But we're not Tony. So we just gave it its own paragraph. And we centered it.

But it's an important point. You are on your own in this industry. And while we have all heard the story of "the girl whose cousin was in the mail room at Warner Bros. and she slipped him her script and he slipped it to his boss who got it to a development exec there who *flipped* for it and handed it to her boss and that girl sold her first script for $1 million," the truth is, that shit never happens. Okay, maybe once in a super-rare while. But it didn't happen to us. And it probably won't happen to you. So forget about that. That is the cavalry. And the cavalry isn't coming. What do you do instead? Funny you should ask. We have a step-by-step process for you. Tony . . . take it away!

STEP I: THE $5 SHORT FILM

Make as many of these as possible, on weekends, with your friends as cast and crew. Use your iPhone camera if that's all you have. Surround yourself with smart, nice people. They don't have to be professional filmmakers (our $3 short film *This Is John,* which got into Sundance, was about as nonprofessional as it gets). Start making five-minute short films that are composed solely of one long scene, starring just two people, set in a single location. Focus only on the story and the performances for now. This singularity of focus will help you distill what you are good at without being overwhelmed by the normal distractions of more complex filmmaking.

Now, if you're anything like us, this first short film will suck. Badly. Some people make a great one right out of the gate. We were not so lucky. Or talented. We suffered many years of bad filmmaking before we made something watchable. But this is okay.

When you are finished with this short, show it to a group of your most honest friends. The ones who aren't afraid to tell you what they really think. Chances are, four minutes and fifty-eight seconds of that short are absolute garbage. But there may be a few inspired seconds of footage in there that one of your friends points out. Focus on those moments. Throw the rest out. Make another short the next weekend. Maybe that one is a little better. Throw out the garbage. Make another one.

And keep going until you make something that feels uniquely like you. Most likely, the tone of the film you're trying to make will have something to do with those intimate, specific late-night conversations you have with a friend or loved one, laughing or crying about something deeply personal. Some would call that your "vision." We would call it your juice. Actually, that sounds disgusting when we write it out. Whatever. Point is, do not stop until you've made an inspired five-minute short (ideally comedic, as film festivals like to program comedic shorts under five minutes). It doesn't have to be pretty. Or polished. Or "professional." It just has to have a spark of truth and originality to it. You'll know it when you've made it. If you have to ask if it's good enough, it's definitely not good enough. Go make another one.

STEP 2: FILM FESTIVALS

While you were making your short films on the weekends, you were working hard at a day job and saving all of your money. You were not eating dinners out. You were borrowing your friend's Netflix password. You were sharing a shitty apartment with way too many other broke-ass people so that you could keep rent at a bare minimum. Let's face it, you have to live cheaply for a long time if you really want to make a go of this career. You have to save for the times when you'll be making movies and not making money. This is one of those times. And the money you have saved will be spent mostly on film festival application fees for your inspired but cheap-as-hell-looking new short film. You should enter it into every film festival that seems decent. Look online for lists of the most prominent (they change constantly). And when you are accepted to a slew of them (and you will be) you have to travel there whenever possible. Sometimes they pay to fly you there, sometimes they don't. Save some money for flights. Most likely the festival will hook you up with a free place to stay and free food while you're there. But just to be safe, also try to walk away with a shit-ton of energy bars from a festival sponsor.

More important, during the period you're traveling to these festivals, you will be writing your feature-length script. It's important that this script have a similar tone and feel to your short. You want people who liked your short to see how the feature will be a natural extension of that short. This will give them confidence to come help you make your movie. And how are you going to get the money to make this feature? Simple. You will pay for it yourself. You will not wait for anyone to give you money. Because you'll wait forever. You will write this feature using the principles of what we call the "available materials" school of filmmaking. That means that this script should have no more than two or three main characters, be easy and cheap to shoot, and be written specifically to utilize the things you have at your disposal. Does your friend's dad own a broken four-wheeler? Great! Write it in. Your mom works at a local diner? Write it in (shoot after hours). Also at your apartment, your friends' apartments, that park nearby where you can shoot at night without permits and no one will notice. You get the picture. This movie should also be shot on your iPhone or a similar cheap camera, using no-name actors and a tiny crew of friends. It should cost no more than $1,000 of your hard-earned savings. And it should have a similar vibe to that $5 short film you made that everyone is loving. And please don't scoff at the iPhone as camera. Our movie *Tangerine* was shot on an iPhone (look it up to see an example of how far a movie shot like this can go).

And at the end of six months of traveling around in support of your short film (in between coming home and still working that day job), you will be connected with a ton of film festivals, you will have bonded with other filmmakers who are willing to work with you on your new project for free, and you will go into production on your first feature film.

STEP 3: THE $1,000 FEATURE FILM

This one will likely hurt a little bit. Your friends may get a little tired of doing you favors by working for free. They know the "backend" you are offering is likely not going to amount to anything because the movie most likely won't sell. They may even want to go off and make their own movies. You will also struggle personally. You'll have to take off work for a few weeks to shoot it (you may even lose your day job and have to find a new one when you wrap your film). You will be doing soooooo many jobs on set yourself. Sleep will be . . . you might not sleep a lot. But if you follow that spirit of your first $5 short film, you will most likely make something that is a bit flawed (it's your first feature!) but inspired and showing a ton of promise. You very well might go to Sundance and sell it for $1 million. In which case . . . congrats! We are jealous and we hate you! You did it so quickly and so much better than we did it.

If not, never fear. It just means that you are a human being. The good news is, even though you didn't get into Sundance with this one, your film has its merits; the film festivals you played with your previous short film remember you and loved hanging with you on your last tour, so they may program your feature. And because very few feature films each year actually work well as a ninety-minute piece, you will likely generate some buzz and get an agent from this $1,000 feature film. And this agent will tell you that he can't wait for you to come to L.A. and take a bunch of general meetings. To put you up for directing gigs. In short, he will tell you that THE CAVALRY IS COMING! And it might . . . but mostly likely it won't. Most likely you'll have a well-reviewed small movie that no one bought or maybe got some small distribution but didn't get you paid. And this will feel like a bit of a letdown.

But you are smart. And you are determined. You know that at these film festivals there are always five to ten movie stars there supporting their bigger-budgeted independent movies. So you socialize with them, befriend them, and get them to see your movie. And you tell your agent that they shouldn't waste their time sending you on general meetings with studios and producers that amount to nothing (remember, make movies, not meetings). You ask them to send a screener of your $1,000 first feature to every single actor represented by your agency who might add "financial value" to your movie. That is, someone who might make buyers want to buy your next movie because that actor's face on the poster brings in viewers.

And when you get home from film festival touring with this first $1,000 feature, you will ask for Skype meetings with every single actor who has responded to your movie in a positive way. And during these Skype meetings you will boldly say to these kind-of-famous actors, "We should go make a thousand-dollar feature together." And most of them will not want to do this with you, because they want to get paid. And they are too used to sitting in trailers on their phones between takes. Which is a bummer but understandable.

However, you will no doubt eventually find that one actor with whom you connect. It may very well be the guy who has been on a ridiculously terrible network procedural drama for ten years. He may not be the dream cast you have been waiting for. His name may even be Randy Hercules. But Randy Hercules is now rich and doesn't need money, he is depressed and creatively bereft from his TV show, and when you tell him you want to build a small, personal movie completely around him and collaborate with him to create his dream leading role, he is going to fall in love with you and follow you to the ends of the earth. And now you have just signed a huge TV star to your next movie. Congrats.

STEP 4: THE $1,000 FEATURE FILM. AGAIN.
WITH RANDY HERCULES

You will get your filmmaker friends to crew one more time for you. Why? Because now you have Randy Hercules. And Randy adds "value" to your movie (a gross term, but we all have to eat, so you should get used to thinking like a producer sometimes). And chances are you will sell this movie for a huge profit. And because communism is an awesome model for an indie film, you will share tons of your backend with your five- or six-person wrecking crew, who have been with you for the past couple of years. At least ten percent for each person. And you will offer Randy maybe twenty percent of the backend, and then secretly ask him to return it so you can share more with the crew, who really need it. And Randy will do it because you inspire him and he wants to feel young and creative again. And he's rich as balls and doesn't care about money.

And when you shoot this movie, you will be more experienced. And you will know how to get that desperate, sad, strange side of Randy to shine onscreen. Everyone will feel it on set. It'll be hard, but you'll all know a reward is coming.

And when you premiere at an even-higher-tier festival, you will sell your movie this time. For no less than $50,000 (because Randy is in it and it's good) but for possibly as high as $500,000 or even more, because Randy could actually get some unexpected nominations (or his TV show was so big in Germany and Russia that sales to those territories alone are worth a quarter of a million dollars). Either way, you have now paid some money to your crew, and you have made enough to quit your day job for a long while (ideally forever) and travel around with your film. This is a fantastic time. Live it up. You worked hard.

And now your agent is freaking out again. You know why? Because he knows now that THE CAVALRY IS COMING! He realizes he already said this once, but now he believes that with this movie you no longer have to sweat it out on the self-funded indie scene. He can probably get you real meetings with producers and studios where you can sell your next movie idea. Or even better, get you into TV, where the real money is! And you will be so excited. Because you have worked your ass off. And *finally* you can relax a little and let the cavalry take you for a ride.

STEP 5: A SMALL STEP BACK

This is the time you let your agent take over. And you do end up selling a TV show idea—possibly even with Randy attached to star—to a major network. They pay you pretty well (though not as well as you'd imagined) to write the pilot. And then . . . you spend a year doing free rewrites for them while they try to make up their minds about what kind of show they want on the air. And you start to realize that as crazy as this sounds, you might have made more money on your tiny Randy Hercules movie than you are making on this TV writing job because of how long it's taking and how many rewrites they are making you do for free. Even worse, by the end of this rewrite process, you may not even recognize the creative tenor of your show anymore. It may be a shadow of the idea you pitched them. And it will have happened slowly, inch by inch, without you even realizing it. And then neither you nor the network nor Randy will like this show, so they will likely put you into "turnaround." Which is a place where great ideas go to die.

This will break you. But just a little. Because you were

smart enough to read the tea leaves on where this whole TV show "development" process was headed about six months ago, and you started developing a *separate* TV show idea on the side. One that worked within the principles of your indie film background (the "available materials" approach). It is something you can shoot an entire episode of on your own dime, with a portion of your profits from the little Randy Hercules movie sale. And you cast Randy's famous actor friend . . . Dingleberry Jones . . . you cast her in this independent TV pilot. (Ms. Jones loved Randy's movie, wanted to meet, and you guys also hit it off.)

And when this pilot is done, you tell your agent to send it to every single TV studio in town, especially the smaller, hungry ones that normally can't compete with the bigwigs. The bigwigs all pass, but a small company makes you an offer to do nine more of these episodes for a full season! The money is not traditionally huge TV money, but it's a great living. And now you have some extra cash. And you're making exactly the kind of show you want to make because you have already set the tone with your pilot, and you have final cut on your episodes because you own the show and made it on your own.

And as you're working away on your new show, something interesting starts to happen. Your friends who used to crew for you all have great movie ideas of their own. And they want the "$1,000 plus a Randy Hercules–type actor" kit to make their own movie. And though you never planned on being a "producer," you suddenly find yourself in a position to connect your friends with both money and a name actor because of all the hard work you've put in. So you do this. Because you like them as people and want to raise them up. Because it is the right thing to do after all they've done for you.

And because you are a good little communist indie film-maker, you don't ask for half of that filmmaker's backend like most financiers do. You only ask to make your money back and for maybe twenty percent of their profits should they sell the movie. And you let your friends share the remainder of the backend with *their* crew. So everyone can make rent and have a healthy indie film ecosystem.

And as you finish making your ten episodes of indie TV, after the trades have commended you for your brash new way of producing television and the industry is getting "hot" on you again, your agent will call you for a heart-to-heart. He will say, "Remember that time I said the cavalry was coming and it didn't come? And that other time I said it was coming and it didn't come? Well . . . now THE CAVALRY IS FUCKING BEATING DOWN YOUR DOOR!" And this time he may be right. Kind of.

STEP 6: A BIG DECISION

Here's the truth. Your agent really does have some genuine-looking opportunities to create something within the Holly-wood system now. A movie idea that a studio wants you to rewrite and direct. Or another TV network that would likely buy a pitch from you to develop a new idea with them. But the brutal reality is, even though it feels like that golden cavalry is right there on your doorstep, it really . . . isn't. That cavalry is still not coming. Because even if you get that rewrite job, they likely won't let you make your movie your way. And even if you sell another TV pitch, you could end up in turnaround again. This is a sobering acknowledgment. A true bummer. That dream you have been working toward, of becoming a "successful filmmaker" who gets studio paychecks, is not what you thought it would be.

So you take stock of your life and try to figure out what went wrong. You've made two feature films, one well reviewed and one with Randy Hercules that did quite well financially and critically. And you've also run a small TV show for a year and produced a few smaller indie films that did well for everyone (some made money, some broke even, but it all balanced out). You are not rich, but you are making a living and you are proud of your work. And you can't help but think . . . "How is it possible, after all these years of hard work and pushing the boulder up the mountain, that the cavalry still isn't coming? How is it possible that I am still funding and creating my own stuff from the ground up after all this time?"

And then it hits you: Who gives a shit about the cavalry? You don't need them. Because now . . . you are the cavalry. Sorry, have to Tony Robbins this one just a little bit.

YOU ARE THE CAVALRY.

Think about it for a second. You are your very own infrastructure. You can self-fund all the micro-budgeted movies and TV shows you want at this point, and you can have full creative control over what you want them to be. And while it is a limit to only make "small" stuff, you can go to bed at night knowing that everything you have made and will make is something that you are proud of, that is reflective of your spirit, and you can show it to your kids one day without explaining why you had to sell out to make it.

This realization is what "making it" means to us now. Being

in independent film and TV is no longer a means to an end to get to Hollywood. It is a way of making things that we believe in and choose to stay with.

So, dear pupils, we humbly say to you: If you can accept that the cavalry probably isn't coming but that you can be your own cavalry, this will be your best chance at maintaining long-term success in your career. Perhaps more important (and something we don't talk enough about in this business), this will give you the best chance at happiness.

TOP 10 FILMS OF ALL TIME (PART 4)*

Gridlocked at twelve, we set a couple of hours aside in our office attic (the creative space) to finalize the list. We bandied around a few solutions, mostly just different cowardly justifications that avoided us actually reducing it to the ten films. Because it was clear that neither of us was ever going to budge. We didn't realize it at the time, but each of us was waiting for the other to be the bigger brother and be the first to knock one of his favorites from the list. The unspoken assumption was that once one of us took that brave first step, the other would quickly follow and we would settle nicely into our final Top 10 list. After all, this was just a fun exercise for the book. There were no real stakes here.

But that didn't happen. And, oddly, things got a bit tense. And quiet. And we started changing the subject. When we ran out of the time we had allotted to figure out this portion of the book, one of us quickly suggested that we drop this series of chapters altogether. That it was trivial and somewhat false. Strangely, neither of us actually *wanted* to drop it. Strangely, we sat in silence, heels dug in like stubborn preteens. Strangely, this stupid exercise was turning out to be a real problem. We left the meeting with twelve movies on our Top 10 list. And no discernible way forward.

American Movie	Dumb and Dumber
Raising Arizona	The Cruise
Tootsie	Henry Fool
Rocky	The Horse Boy
Hoop Dreams	You Can Count On Me
The Crying Game	Close-Up

* *To be continued . . .*

X.

Before Mark and I shot a frame of our little feature film *The Puffy Chair,* we set a few unorthodox filmmaking rules to better our chances of making a feature that didn't suck this time around. They were, in no particular order:

Keep it small. Once word got out that we were making a new feature, our reputation in the tiny world of independent film was big enough to attract offers from people wanting to come with us, even willing to chip in for free on the crew. But as exciting as it sounded to have more bodies and more help, we couldn't forget about the bloated *Vince Del Rio* set and how it often distracted us from the task at hand: Get good performances and good story. And while it may have been a bit overprotective of us to turn away such generous free labor, we felt strongly that we should stay lean and mean. We were simply not confident in our ability to make a good film if there was too much noise around and too many other jobs to focus on. Story. Acting. We promised to let everything else go for now.

Another rule was to blow off the schedule if needed. While we had allotted eighteen shoot days, we would not make the same mistake of forcing ourselves to "make our days." This is what got us into the most trouble on *Vince Del Rio* . . . trying to please our crew and producers by being good little Catholic boys who followed the rules. To be clear, this didn't mean that we could shoot for a hundred days and just be lazy about it, but it did mean we promised that if we got to a point on set where we needed a little bit more time to get things right, we would take that time and get the scene right. Even if it meant punting a scene to the next day so we could rewrite or even reconceive it, we would allow ourselves to fail and regroup. If there is one lesson we have learned from being on set it is that if you are sitting there asking yourself, "Did we get it?" then it most certainly means you did not get it. And while it's never fun to reschedule or "go over," in the end everyone will thank you for taking the time to be honest about what's not working and then get it right. (NOTE: Another benefit of keeping our crew small was that if we went over, it wouldn't be a huge expense and upheaval of an existing machine's order.)

Lastly, we decided to shoot the film in its natural scene order. When making a film, it is much more practical to shoot the scenes out of chronological sequence. For instance, if three scenes in the movie take place in one restaurant, you go there and shoot all three scenes in a row. Cheaper, more efficient, smarter all around. For *Puffy*, we decided to shoot the film in the exact order that the scenes took place in the film. This often meant asking actors to hang around production longer than they needed to, or even doubling back on locations. But because we used our "available materials" school of filmmaking, this wasn't a big ask of the locations, which were mostly given to us for free. The big benefit to this approach was being able to track the organic relationship dynamics as they progressed in real time. While we do work from a traditional script, we often improvise the dialogue on set so that we can make things feel more natural. By shooting in chrono-logical order, if something interesting came up in the improv, we could incorporate that surprise into the subsequent scenes (which is impossible to do when you are shooting out of sequence). We could now look at a fight scene we shot the previous night and say things like, "He was more defensive than we thought he would be, so he should be aware of that in this apology scene and be a bit more contrite than we initially imagined." It was a perfect way to dial in the nuances of the interpersonal dynamics that make or break small films like the one we were making. And this is an approach we still use whenever possible.

With these basic tenets in place, we shot the first two days in Mark's apartment in New York City, and they went off with-out a hitch. Feeling confident and inspired, the six of us hopped into the van and started our drive up to Maine. Along the way, we shot a simple scene in which Emily (played by Katie) has to go to the bathroom, but Josh (played by Mark) won't stop driving because he wants to make good time on the road. It was a classic road movie conflict, and we played it in a fun, subtle way that alluded to some of the darkness that ex-isted beneath the surface of Josh and Emily's seemingly fun relationship. In short, we felt we nailed it. We were so excited to see what we came up with that we pulled out the tapes that night and gathered in one of our shared Motel 6 rooms to preview the magic.

The footage, however, was completely unusable. The cam-era had developed a bug in transit, and the whole day's shoot-ing was a bust. Not only was it disheartening to lose what we thought was a great scene, we couldn't shoot the next day be-cause our camera was broken. After a few hours on the phone trying to get it fixed, we realized that we would have to break out the credit cards and buy a brand-new camera, shelling out hundreds extra to have it overnighted so we would only lose one day of shooting. Our hope was to get the broken camera fixed after the shoot and then eBay it to defray the cost of the new camera, which we felt confident we could rent out again over the next year to pay off. Not a huge deal, but a blow to the momentum for sure.

Still, that strange down day off the interstate in Bangor, Maine, was a tough one. We were all feeling a sense of doom. That our movie might be somehow cursed. That the underdog momentum we had been building since our first Sundance short in 2003 might be hitting a wall.

And the next day was a little bit worse, when we got the new camera and reshot the "pee scene," as we called it. Because this time around, the scene was uninspired, false, and forced. And we all felt it. Katie and Mark tried their hardest to get back that fun spark of the first time around, but it was gone. We hammered away at it for twelve hours and eventually flopped into the van and made our way to Milbridge for the rest of the shoot.

When we got to Milbridge, we settled into a groove. Mark, Katie, and Rhett found their characters' voices and drilled into them. I was operating the camera, directing, and running sound right into the camera, so I was exhausted at the end of every day. But we were getting good footage, and it felt like it was working.

The hardest part of the shoot for Mark and me was learning how to collaborate closely with others. This was the beginning of a long journey that we still struggle with today. We tend to communicate in gestures, grunts, odd references. And this was all fine when we were making a $3 short in our kitchen with just the two of us, but we now needed to include

Rhett and Katie in this dialogue, and we were admittedly not very good at it. Add into this mix the fact that Katie and Mark were dating at the time (and all the meta stuff going on in the scenes and their relationship), and the soup started to become somewhat insane.

As often happens on set, allegiances started to build. Mark and Katie, as a couple and as the main actors in the film, had built a sometimes impenetrable bond as scene partners that I often found hard to crack. This was a shock to me, since it had always been Mark and me against the world. Likewise, Katie often felt left out of the bizarre inner communication circle of Mark and me as directors of the film. To make matters even worse, she and I often commiserated and joined forces against Mark's fast-paced type-A bedside manner. It was like a complex game of *Survivor,* where alliances were made and broken on an hourly basis. And while there were never any big fights about it, it was definitely a confusing time for all of us and a big learning curve for Mark and me as brothers in terms of letting other people into the twinlike fold we had built over the past twenty-five years.

The good news was that despite these challenges and conflicts (or perhaps because of them), we stayed on our toes and gave everything we had to the movie. We improvised when it wasn't right, we took walks and rewrote when scenes felt stilted, and Katie even pulled out an improvised rewrite for the end of the film that in our opinion makes the movie what it is today. And after our twenty-one production days (yep, we went three days over schedule, and it was worth it), we all came out alive and felt we had something special in the can. We said goodbye to Milbridge and to Katie's parents (who had become parents to all of us during the shoot) and headed back to Brooklyn to edit the film.

The first thing we noticed in editing was that, as we expected, the "pee scene" was just not inspired. In fact, the whole first fifteen minutes of the movie seemed to be suffering a little bit. Once Josh and Emily got on the road, the movie really took off, but something was just off in that early footage. We tried to diagnose it and treat it a bunch of different ways, and then began to ask that wonderfully naïve question of ourselves: "Maybe we're being too hard on it and it's fine?"

Relying on our proven process for audience feedback, we gathered a group of filmmakers and smart friends to watch a rough cut of the movie. And, of course, the first act of the film was just not landing. This was a huge blow because we once again found ourselves in the familiar position of having a quality issue and not knowing how to fix it (*Vince Del Rio* all over again). But this time we felt that the overall quality of the movie was worth sticking with and trying to fix. So we hunkered down. Mark did what he usually does, which is avoid reshooting at all costs. He is very resistant to it and wanted to make the fix somehow in editorial. I, for whatever reason, am much more willing to reopen production, and I began pushing hard for not only reshoots but rewrites as well. Essentially my idea was to completely reconceive the first fifteen minutes. I dragged Mark into it, and once I did it was obvious to us both that this was the right way to go.

Then something great happened. We were forced to truly ask, "What is wrong with this couple?" and "What is their journey?" By having already shot the film, we realized we now had a chance to reverse engineer our beginning to perfectly fit the film . . . which was already shot. It was a small concept but proved to be a huge breakthrough.

One night shortly after this realization, while we were

brainstorming in Mark's apartment, *Lethal Weapon* came on TV and gave us an idea. They start the movie with a generic action scene to get the story going before all the boring setup and exposition. We looked at each other and said nothing. We started improvising a "right out of the gate" fight scene between Josh and Emily that was indicative of their issues. Our version of that nonspecific action scene from *Lethal Weapon*. We came up with a scene that featured Josh and Emily being passive-aggressive, using their trademark baby talk to deal with each other. Josh was trying to get some distance from Emily, to go on this road trip alone. But he was afraid to ask. This made her fearful that he was pulling away and caused her to glom on to him more tenaciously. We improvised this concept a bit as the two of us happened to be eating chicken, so we just decided to write the chicken dinner right into the scene for Josh and Emily. We were so excited we were dancing around the room like idiots. But we stayed in it and hunkered down to finish the rest of the rewrite. We knew we needed another scene to bring them back together, to show the *good* side of their relationship before they took off on the trip. We thought about it awhile and started talking about Lloyd Dobler, from the movie *Say Anything . . .* , and how awesome he was. How he could make mistakes, but he was such a loving dude you couldn't help but forgive him. We lamented that we hadn't thought of the iconic Peter Gabriel ghetto blaster scene ourselves. And then it hit us . . . Josh is the kind of guy who would love Lloyd. He is of a generation that just wants to be Lloyd. Let's have Josh reenact the ghetto blaster scene for Emily and win her back.

Careful not to lose the momentum, we set up the reshoots right away. We knew enough then to know that whenever you can shoot a scene that you are still in love with due to its freshness, it has that much better of a chance to be great. So we shot the new scenes within the week and then picked up some extra road footage to help sell the travel element of the movie (we hadn't done a good job of this in production). Within two days, Jay Deuby had edited the scenes in, and just like that the movie emerged.

We held a test screening in the basement of Two Boots Pizza on the Lower East Side of Manhattan and invited forty filmmakers and friends. We sat in back as usual and watched them watch the movie. Within ten minutes we knew the film was working. When it was over everyone told us how much they related to Josh and Emily and their journey. How it felt like we had put a microphone in their apartment and recorded the last fight they'd had with their significant other.

We rode the subway home that night. There was a lot of smiling and grabbing of each other's knees. And high-fiving. And a shitload of crying. We had finally cracked a feature film that worked. And we had done it on our own, in our way. It was a massive breakthrough.

From: jay duplass
To: mark duplass
Subject: xmas eve

dupes. that was an awesome night. I feel like everyone was at their best. mom and dad. the kids were just jamming together and loving it all. it just worked. thx for hosting that and ushering it into being.

———————

From: mark duplass
To: jay duplass
Subject: RE: xmas eve

I felt it too. I thought about it a lot after u guys left and was trying to crack the code to why it worked so well. I guess sometimes things just have an energy and u get lucky or whatever. but I wish we could bottle it or map it out in some way to help re-create it cuz it was so rad and beautiful. particularly with me and u and jen and katie. did u notice that?

———————

From: jay duplass
To: mark duplass
Subject: RE: xmas eve

yeah. that was the biggest part for me. i've always convinced myself that i had unrealistic expectations of how close u and me and our wives would all be. like we would all live in a commune and share all the same ideals and raise our kids together kinda thing. obviously it's more complex than that and my brain can totally accept it, but in my heart I still feel badly that it doesn't just click in perfectly like I hoped it would.

_____

From: mark duplass
To: jay duplass
Subject: RE: xmas eve

dude. dupiss face johnson. thank u for having the heart and balls to say that. I have been wanting to broach this subject for a long time and have been kinda scared to say it. and u just kinda blew it open for me and I'm really glad u did. can I just say . . .

I wish u and katie were closer and I wish me and jen were closer.

I know we love each other and it works but . . . I wish what u wished too. I wish we were all soul mates.

_____

From: jay duplass
To: mark duplass
Subject: RE: xmas eve

ha! me too. I totally feel you on this. it sucks. and I don't know how to fix it.

_____

From: mark duplass
To: jay duplass
Subject: RE: xmas eve

me neither. but I'm glad we're talking about it. and I'm glad we had a rad xmas eve together where it all came straight out of the oven like we imagined it would when we wrote the cookbook, sleeping in our twin bed together 35 years ago.

_____

From: jay duplass
To: mark duplass
Subject: RE: xmas eve

maybe we can talk a little before we do these bigger family get-togethers and try to plant some seeds of fun. ie, I think the little singalong thing u did at the piano helped to set the mood.

some ideas:
—as the kids get older, sharing seminal movies together that we all loved as a family. raising arizona, rocky, hoosiers.

—big charade game with interfamily teams
(I'm already hating these ideas and they feel forced. probably can't control this and just have to get lucky.)

last idea: get mom really stoned and just sit in the corner and watch her.

YOU (AN EXERCISE IN EMPATHY)

PART 2

You ARE A woman. You are twenty-seven years old. You are overweight. You wear a poly-blend light pink hooded sweatshirt that says "U Maine" on the front and a pair of men's mesh basketball shorts. These clothes are very comfortable. You changed into them a half hour ago from your work uniform. You work at Kentucky Fried Chicken, which is what you also ate for dinner tonight. Like last night. You make $15,492 per year as a fry cook. You also make $598 a month from the state of Maine welfare system. You are underpaid, but you keep your job at KFC because the benefits are good. Because you have three children under the age of nine. And because you take care of them by yourself after your dickless husband, Chad, ran off with your hairdresser, whose name is Stacy but everyone calls Pumpkin because of her big, round, gushy ass.

Tonight you are very, very tired. Like last night. But tonight there is a *Vikings* marathon on TV that you have been looking forward to. You've actually thought about it somewhat obsessively all day. You just need to get the kids into the bathtub, wash them, get their teeth brushed, help them pick out their outfits for tomorrow, read books to two of them, and make sure the nightlight is perfectly positioned for all three to sleep with, and then you will have one hour to yourself in front of the TV before you fall asleep. It doesn't matter that you fall asleep on the couch, because you live in a small one-bedroom apartment and the kids all share the bedroom. Your bedroom *is* the living room. Your bed is the couch. You know this is all temporary. Actually, you hope this is all temporary.

The children are particularly difficult tonight. You do not know whether it's them or whether you are just tired and impatient. You don't really care. You just need to get them to sleep as quickly as possible so that you can get to the TV. To see *Vikings*. But your youngest is unrealistic about what her share of the covers should be. She keeps dragging them to her side and robbing her older brother of his share. Your older daughter watches with dead eyes from her sleeping bag on the floor as your son elbows your youngest and she begins to cry, much more loudly and dramatically than the offense justifies. This infuriates you, which in turn scares your children. It stops the conflict but makes you feel worse, that their fear of you is what it took to make them get along. You can't think about this too much. You know these thoughts are not helpful and only make the butterflies in your chest wake up (you often get butterflies in your chest that make you feel nauseated and scared of the world).

At last they fall asleep. At last you plop onto the couch and turn on the TV. But the remote is broken. So you now have to drag your ass off the couch to turn the TV on manually. But, still, the TV doesn't turn on. And now the butterflies are waking up, because you realize there may be something wrong with the TV. You unplug it and plug it back in. Still nothing. You test the plug with a lamp. Shit. The lamp works in the same plug. It's not the plug. You change the remote batteries by stealing some good double A's from your son's remote-control truck. Those good batteries don't make the TV work either.

You become very quiet as the butterflies take over your chest and the fear of the world returns. You begin to cry. And you become angry at yourself that a broken TV can make you cry. So you lay yourself down on the couch and close your eyes. And you will yourself to sleep. To put this day behind you. You lay there for twenty minutes, fighting the butterflies. But you can't win. You try so hard. But they are too strong. And you are too upset about this TV. It was all you wanted to-night, and some . . . someone took it from you.

Strangely, someone inside of you wakes up. A new person. And she starts to tell you that you deserve that TV. That there are new ones at Walmart less than four miles away. That the kids are old enough to sleep alone for thirty minutes while you make a quick run to get a new TV. A big one. So that you can have what you want and deserve. The other people inside of you, the ones that you already know and have known for years, argue with this new person. They tell her that you need to save your money for a down payment on a house, school funds, your children's futures. But those existing people are also fighting the butterflies, so their voices are not as strong and clear as this new voice. This new voice already has you out the door and into your ex-husband's truck, which he left you as a parting gift. This new voice already has you down the road and stopping at the Irving for a forty-eight-ounce Dr Pepper, which you slurp with surprising speed. This new voice ex-plains to you, finally, that your need for these sodas stems from when your father gave them to you when you and he used to dig for mussels at his cousin Joe's house off Wyman. That the sugar and caffeine give you a sense of power and warm love that you desperately need. And this all makes sense to you as you park the truck and bathe in the warmth of Walmart's famous entrance heaters that always say, "Welcome and come in and get your comfort because it's right here inside."

And you don't have to wander, because you know where the TVs are, and for the first time you don't even look at prices or coupons. You simply find the biggest TV in the whole place and you ask for it to be put into your car. And you pay for it with cash. A whole month's worth of welfare and then some. And the existing people inside of you are screaming at you and begging you not to do this, or at the very least to wait a minute and look at the prices and the coupons, but the butterflies have nearly drowned them out by now. And this new person inside is laughing and cheering and telling you how brave you are and how hard you work and how much you deserve everything you are getting for yourself.

And as you drive home, way over the speed limit, you finish your soda and throw the empty cup out the window at Pumpkin's house. You throw that thing right out the window, just like your father used to do, and it feels good to be like him for a moment. It feels good to drive fast and throw shit and dream about all the fun you'll have with your new TV that you've worked so fucking hard for.

And you walk in the door and you see your younger daughter sobbing on the couch, screaming for her mother. And you see your son staring at you with a look of utter disappointment and confusion. And then you see the oldest. Your nine-year-old. The one who is most like you. And she is angry. And she comes at you, yelling, calling you names and accusing you of being a terrible, terrible mother for leaving your children home alone. And you are staring at a younger version of yourself who is about to attack you and right now you just hate yourself, so before you know it you raise your right hand and slap her so hard that she hits the floor. And something about the noise of the slap and the look of betrayal on her face seems to neutralize that new person inside of you. And zap the butterflies. And you can see clearly what has happened over the past thirty-five minutes. You see it from the viewpoint of the existing people inside of you. The people who have been with you your whole life. And it looks bad. It looks and feels so bad. And you don't know what you should do, but you do know that you are too far along this waterslide to try to climb back up. That maybe the smartest (or only) move you have at this point is to let go and cascade as quickly as you can to the bottom. To splash into the cold pool below. And then, somehow, try to pick yourself up and drag your ass all the way back up those stairs to the top of the slide. And try it again tomorrow.

XI.

HAVING YOUR SHORT film premiere at Sundance is incredibly exciting, but there is nothing quite like the moment when they call and tell you that your first feature film has been accepted. In November 2004, Jay and I got the call from a friend that we'd barely squeaked into the festival lineup with *The Puffy Chair*. We later learned that the head programmer at the time thought the film sucked but that all the younger programmers really liked it and pushed us through.

This is when our careers really started.

A feature film is something that can save you from being broke as shit. Which is what we were at the time and what we were looking to not be anymore. The previous Sundance had seen the $4 million sale of a small film called *Napoleon Dynamite*. Since we had made *The Puffy Chair* for $10,000 with a loan from our parents, we couldn't help but wonder: "What if we are the breakout hit of Sundance? Is it possible that someone is going to buy our film for a multimillion-dollar price tag?" Stranger things had happened, so we both went in with cautious optimism and fairly intense cases of diarrhea.

In a random act of programming cruelty, our film wouldn't premiere until an entire week after the festival began. So we waited. Impatiently. As other films popped and got bought.

And others fizzled and disappeared. It was torture, but finally our premiere came on a Wednesday night at the Library Center Theatre (now our favorite theater in Park City). We tribed up with our parents and Katie in the middle of the sold-out crowd and waited anxiously to see if we got that first laugh. We knew that if we didn't get it, it meant the audience wasn't going to like our film and we'd be in for a long ninety minutes. Then something crazy happened . . . they laughed *before* the first laugh in the film. At something super subtle and nuanced. We all looked at one another and burst into tears. And watched as our movie played through the roof. Our Q&A session was a total lovefest. Buyers, agents, managers, producers, and studio executives were all swarming us and the film's sales agents. It was the moment we had been waiting for. It was utterly surreal. We could feel it. We were going to be the breakout movie!

And then . . . things slowed down a bit. Everyone certainly loved the movie, but there was some hesitation on the part of buyers to purchase a film that had "no big stars and a rather rough-hewn production value." In many ways, it seemed that everyone wanted to finance our *next* movie, but they were having trouble pulling the trigger on the movie that they so adamantly claimed they were in love with.

So the festival ended. And still the movie hadn't sold. But this wasn't an anomaly. Sometimes it took a bit of time to find the right buyer. Our sales agents kept assuring us that it would all work out eventually, but one by one all the big buyers were passing, and soon we were hoping for any paycheck, let alone a multimillion-dollar sale.

In the meantime, Katie and I (who both starred in the film) decided to go to Los Angeles for a few months to ride the wave of the film's critical popularity. Jay would go back to New York, where we were all living at the time, and take all the East Coast meetings. This was an early example of what would become our "divide and conquer" approach, which we have since mastered. Sort of.

It turned out that most of the business happens in L.A. (go figure), so Jay spent a ton of time flying out there, sleeping on Katie's and my couch, and taking rounds of meetings all over Los Angeles with me. And everywhere we went the message was the same: "We LOVED *The Puffy Chair*. What's your next movie? We want to make it!" It all seemed so simple. We had literally hundreds of options of producers and studios who all seemed to be clamoring to make our next film.

During this time, we were also traveling to film festivals around the world in support of *The Puffy Chair*. And while those festivals would pay for our travel, put us up, and feed us, we certainly weren't making any money, and we had yet to pay back our parents' $10,000 loan for the movie. In short, we seemed to be in demand, but we couldn't figure out how to actually make money.

So we started pitching new movie ideas. And we took a TV show idea around town that was about my life in bands. All the TV studios who'd said, "We want your next project," rejected it. As it turned out, they didn't want our next project, they just wanted the *option* to buy our next project. Which meant that we would pitch them an idea, they would turn it down, and they would then ask to buy our *next* one after that. Rinse and repeat. We also were approached to rewrite some of the studios' broken scripts that they had in their back catalogue and were looking to breathe new life into. To bring that "honest, raw, emotional comedy" to it that we had put into *The Puffy Chair*. Great! We'll do that! So we took their broken scripts and made pitches to deepen them. Make them, ideally, more true and honest. Those pitches were also rejected. As most of those pitches involved losing the very ridiculous set pieces that were making the scripts broken in the first place. It seems they were all for emotional honesty, as long as we didn't get rid of the "diarrhea out the fourth-floor window" set piece.

Meanwhile, almost all of the buyers had passed on *The Puffy Chair* by now, and six months had elapsed since Sundance. It was starting to look like an old film that no one wanted to buy. We weren't able to get any jobs in L.A. And all the noise around us was starting to quiet.

So we started to panic. I, in particular, became afraid that if we didn't act quickly we would lose our momentum. We both were looking to build a normal life with our girlfriends. Get married. Find a way to make money. And it all seemed to be slipping away.

Then, in late fall 2005, we finally got a legitimate offer on *The Puffy Chair*. And it was good, $150,000. It included a TV sale and a nice DVD release. But it wouldn't go into theaters. Our sales agent and good friend Liesl Copland presented it to us, and without blinking we both said, "WE'LL TAKE IT." But she urged us to pause. She did have one more offer for us to consider. It was a combined offer for a small (at the time) but reputable theatrical company called Roadside Attractions and a new digital-space pioneer called Netflix that was renting DVDs through the mail. This offer would take our movie into theaters, get it reviewed, and give us a chance as directors to really pop in the world. It would be more of an investment in our future. Painfully, it was a "no advance" offer. This meant that we got no money upfront but would share the profits if the film was a success.

And it hit us like a ton of bricks. We had $150,000 on the

table with that first offer. The chance to pay back our parents. To share the rest of the profits with our cast and crew. Rent money for at least two years if we lived cheaply. It offered so much. But Liesl knew, and we knew deep down, that we had to take the long play. We had to go with Roadside Attractions and Netflix. Roadside would put us in theaters. Netflix would advertise us on the inside of their DVD mailer envelopes. They were even discussing getting into the business of streaming their movies online, and we could be pioneers in that space with them.

So with heavy, sad hearts, we turned down the $150,000 (FUCK YOOOOUUUUUUUU!) and went with the Roadside/Netflix deal. It almost killed us to do it. But even our parents, who would have to wait over a year to get paid back, were supportive of the move. And in the end, Liesl was right. What those companies did in terms of getting our film into the world and our names along with it proved to be invaluable in launching our careers. And even though the money part was tough to give up, we ultimately made more on the backend due to how well the film performed, particularly on Netflix's new streaming service.

We were feeling emboldened. We were feeling that indie film would take care of us if we stayed true to it. That we didn't need Hollywood one bit. And then, because life is a strange person with many strange hats, within two weeks of this realization we were offered our first deal to write and direct a multimillion-dollar feature film with a major studio.

SOME THOUGHTS ON
LYING

THERE'S A MOMENT that happens on nearly every film set. The sun is going down. The day is coming to a close. Everyone has been working for eleven hours. Time is running out. And there is still one more scene to shoot. And everyone knows that there is not enough time to shoot the scene. Or at least shoot it properly. This is the point where the director, profusely sweating and stressed out to the core, approaches the cast and puts on a fairly convincing smile. . . .

"So I've been thinking about this scene and . . . I know we discussed shooting this from both sides in a variation of close-ups, medium shots, dolly and Steadicam moves, but . . . the more I think about it, that might be overkill. And . . . I'm thinking . . . it might actually be *more* poignant if we just back off and shoot it all in one big wide shot? Just . . . one shot. You know? Kinda, just . . . let the words and you guys as actors do your thing and I'll just stay out of the way. Right?"

The director puts it out there. And everyone knows that this director, in this moment, is full of shit. Because everyone has been here before. Everyone knows that there is only one hour left to shoot before we go into overtime and that the only *possible* version of the scene is the one the director just pitched. That this new plan has nothing to do with "vision" or "choice" and is merely a desperate attempt to finish the day on schedule.

So the cast members take their turn next. And put on *their* fake smiles . . .

"I kinda love that idea."

"Yeah, man. It's cool. Kinda like that Woody Allen thing."

"Totally. Let's do this. It's . . . it's definitely better."

"One hundred percent."

And with that, everyone heads into the scene. A little more soul-sick than they were a few minutes ago. And it sucks. For everyone. Because it's a lie. And everyone knows it. And everyone is afraid to call out the truth. But the funny thing is, the truth of the situation is actually not that bad if you just lay it on the table without any frills or fake smiles. Imagine for a second if the director had the courage to say something like this:

"Okay, so . . . I'm pretty sure you all know what I'm about to say. It's . . . six P.M. We have to wrap by seven or else we will go into overtime, and we don't have the budget for that. So I know we had this really cool, intricate plan to shoot the scene, but . . . well, that's not happening. That being said, I do think there's an alternate version where we just shoot this in one big wide shot. It's something we can do with the time we have, it'll keep us all on schedule, and . . . who knows? Maybe there will be some accidental poignancy to it? Maybe some reviewer will say, 'I love how the director chose to stay out of the way and let the words and actors do their thing.' Ha! Or not. Maybe it'll just be a compromised version of the scene. And if it is, maybe we can look at it later and see if there's another solution. But for now, this wide-shot plan is what we can do, with our limited time and budget. I apologize for the gear shift, but I'd love it if you guys would join me and give it our all for the next . . . fifty-eight minutes, and see if we can make some lemonade out of these lemons. I have a feeling if we just gear up for it and make the best out of what we have, that we'll find something inspired and interesting. What do you think?"

If we were actors on a set, we would so much prefer to hear this. It's the truth, we can feel sympathy for the director's position, and we can get on board.

So next time you find yourself having that conversation that we continually have with each other—the one where you are asking advice on how to handle a given situation and what "version of the truth" you should tell the person when you next contact him? The whole "I *want* to be his friend and have the occasional lunch with him, but I kinda know he has a little crush on me and I don't see him that way, so I worry that if I *do* accept his invite I'll be leading him on, so I'm not sure what I should tell him . . ." conversation? Try doing what we've been telling each other to do for the past few years:

"You should tell that person *exactly* what you just told me."

Because if that person heard you fumbling through it with all your cards on the table, he would know that you were so thoughtful and considerate of him that you agonized over how to handle his feelings. And he would know that you actively sought out advice as to how to handle it properly. And that, in the end, the situation was so complex that you ultimately couldn't find the clean, elegant solution and that it was tearing you up a bit. If you just said all those things? In short, if you just told the awkward, fumbly, nervous truth . . . we bet that person would feel really good about what you had to say. They would feel considered. They would feel you put time into their feelings. Perhaps most important, they would inherently know that you were telling the truth . . . which is becoming harder and harder to discern these days.

THE BLOWJOB CHRONICLES

WE ONCE HAD a movie idea called *The Blowjob* that we were obsessed with making. It was a small, intimate, sad, darkly
funny story about three characters and how their lives
changed forever with a seemingly small event . . . pun in-
tended. It seemed like it was going to be the follow-up to *The
Puffy Chair*. But for some reason we could never crack it in
ninety-minute form and make it feel like a great feature film.
We wrestled with it for months and eventually had to just let it
go out on an ice floe into the sea of inspired but ultimately
abandoned ideas.

But we love that sea. And have learned that letting ideas go
there doesn't mean they are gone forever. They often come
back with beards, shaved armpits, new tattoos. Sometimes
we don't even recognize them until they start speaking to us
again. Most of the time they return as a new film or a fun side
story line in one of our TV shows. But with this book we have
a new way to resurrect one of our old friends from the dead.
The Blowjob is going to live a new life. Right here. It will be the
first short story we have ever written. And will likely be terrible. But that's okay. Because it's called *The Blowjob*, and it
has at least that going for it already.

Also, so you guys can get a truer sense of how we collaborate, here is the initial vomit draft of the story, as is, along with Jay's first set of feedback notes. Hope you learn something interesting and that the story doesn't suck too badly.

THE BLOWJOB

Paul was sleeping. And so was Maggie. But Alice wasn't. She was bonking. Bonking into the front door of Paul and Maggie's apartment while struggling with her keys. Then, once inside, bonking into the thin drywall opposite Paul and Maggie's bedroom on her way to her room (which was Maggie's office but had served as Alice's temporary room for the past three weeks). Then dropped her phone. Bonking on the crappy parquet floor of Maggie's office. This third bonk is what woke up Maggie.

"You okay, Alice?"   *↳ like this "bonk" runner. lets us know its not taking itself too seriously.*

Quiet.

"Alice?"

More bonking. But mild, muffled bonking. Settling into the covers of the twin sleeper sofa bed kinda bonking.   *maybe overdoing it now?*

"Yep! I'm good! Sorry, Mags!"

Maggie relaxes, and then subconsciously lets fifteen percent of her annoyance seep into her voice.

"Okay. Go to sleep, honey."

"Okay!"   *→ cute*

Maggie rolls over and her mass of semi-dirty but still kinda good-smelling brown curls flops onto Paul's boyish, angular, clean-shaven face. At this point she notices he is also awake.

"Hi."

"Hi."

"What's the plan, Mags?"

"I'm gonna let this one go."

"I think that's a good idea."

"Love you."

"Love you."

like that you're not doing the "he said" "she said" thing but it got confusing for a second here. Let's discuss how to clarify it.

Maggie rolls over and closes her eyes. Paul rolls over and does not close his eyes. For the past three weeks, Alice has been crashing at their tiny Greenpoint railroad apartment in Brooklyn. The sudden death of her long-term boyfriend, Craig, has destroyed almost every inch of her being. Inside and out. The Xanax and alcohol binges are keeping her from exploding into a zillion terrifically sad pieces. But it has been three weeks. And she is still, somehow, descending.

let's beat this cliché

Last week Paul and Maggie sat down with Alice and gave her a loving ultimatum. They were happy to continue helping her with a place to stay and also provide emotional and financial support (she was their mutual best friend since college), but that was predicated on her starting to take steps to help herself. Those steps had not yet been taken by Alice. Thus the state of living in this tiny apartment had fallen into a bit of a stalemate. Paul and Maggie mostly agreed on how to handle this situation, with the one difference being that Paul had a bit more patience—

"MAGS!"

Love the interruption. great idea

A forty-nine percent scared but fifty-one percent

annoyed Maggie throws off the covers and heads into her office/Alice's new bedroom. There she finds Alice in her infamous bright red turtleneck, which seems to hold up her bright red face like a tee does a golf ball. Alice struggles to remove her jeans, wobbling in a sure-fire pre-bonk kinda way. Maggie notices that Alice is terrifically hammered. *nice*

"Can you please not yell in the apartment like that, Alice?" *↳ so good. treats her like a kid*

"I didn't yell. I was calling for you, Mags."

"Fine. Okay. Do you need help with your jeans?"

"What? Why would you ask that?"

Maggie ignores this question and helps Alice unbutton her oversized button-fly boyfriend jeans.

"Lot easier getting these off of Craig than me."

feels Maggie tosses Alice's jeans into a pile of a pile of a *little* *piiiiile* of laundry in the corner and tucks her drunk, *forced* drunk friend into bed. Sofa bed.

"You need to sleep, Alice."

"Mags, I love you. I love you. Not as much as I love Craig. But he's dead. So. Now I just wanna say I love you. Cuz I do. I love you. And I love PAAUUUUL!"

"Alice, the shouting. Paul is sleeping."

"Right!"

Maggie kisses Alice softly on the forehead and heads for the door. By the time she turns to say good night, Alice is almost asleep. Maggie turns off the light and returns to the bedroom, where Paul is still turned over and still not asleep.

"All good in there?"

"Our best friend is twenty-seven years old and headed for a full-on train wreck, Paul."

"Yeah, but her two best friends are also twenty-seven. They are young and smart and capable and dedicated and they are gonna help her keep the train on the track. Now bring me that stinky head of yours, Mags."

"I washed it on Saturday. Does it stink already?"

"Little bit. But good stink. I like the way you stink."

this is a rip-off of Pulp Fiction :) you probably forgot

Maggie lies on Paul. He takes a big, big drink of her moppy curly hair through his big-skinny nose. He is comforted by this little routine. And so is she.

LOVE

LOVE

"PAUL!!!"

Paul shoots up. One hundred percent scared. He sees that it's very late now and that Maggie is asleep next to him, facedown. He immediately thinks that she looks like roadkill under that mass of curls. Then he remembers Craig and regrets the image of roadkill immediately after that first thought.

smart set-up!

Now that Paul is alert enough to know it is just Alice calling for him from the other room, Paul is zero percent scared and one hundred percent sympathetic. It's just his way with Alice. Ever since college. Since they shared lunch together at Gottlieb Cafeteria every day the first semester. And she would ask him to get her things and he would simply get up and get them for her. Without thinking about it. Since he discovered in cultural anthropology class that she was way smarter than him but somehow destined to be way less successful. His spirit somehow aligned with hers. He understood her and she understood him. They never discussed it. They were each other's person.

% analogy not my favorite

don't know why but this name sounds fake to me

"PAUL! C'mere!"

And Paul gets up. Because that's the way Paul is for

Alice. She asks and he does. So he goes into her room and finds her still tucked into her bed. Sofa bed. She smiles. She looks maybe seven years old. And she is less drunk and bonky now.

"I just remembered something."

"What's that, Alice?"

Alice sits up. She still wears her red turtleneck.

"I forgot to pick up Craig's rent deposit."

"I can help you with that tomorrow."

"There's so much shit to do, Paul."

"Yep."

love it
natural
feels real

It's quiet. Alice fiddles with her left pinky for a moment.

"Is that all you wanted to talk about?"

Alice thinks about this. For a long beat. Then one more longer beat.

"His hand was . . . like Play-Doh. Like, flattened-out-with-a-rolling-pin Play-Doh." *fucking great*

Paul winces. But he does not look away. Since Craig's accident, Alice has not spoken about it in any detail. He instinctually knows he has to be here for her and listen. So he goes to the side of her bed. Sofa bed. And sits down. And listens.

LOVE THIS! "I think the back wheels got his left hand when he flopped onto the street. It was like a cartoony kinda joke. A bunch of his inner hand just kinda burst out the tops of his fingers." *yuv're on fire with this shit!*

Alice looks at Paul, and he holds her stare. He is pale and somewhat queasy hearing these details, but he is also listening and he is also here. As she knew he would be.

"I'm not sure I'm gonna make it, Paul."

"Alice. You're gonna be fine. That's crazy."

"I don't feel right. I feel very . . . off."

"That's natural."

"It's not, Paul."

And the way she looks at him suddenly makes Paul deeply, deeply worried for her.

"I need you guys and I'm scared Mags is getting sick of me."

"She's just a little tired. She's fine."

"You're tired. And you don't talk to me the way she does."

"Alice. It's all good. You just need sleep—"

"I've been sleeping for three weeks. I don't need sleep. I need . . ." → *the reader might be a head of you here. Cuz*

Alice trails off. She is quiet. Paul waits. Then . . .

"Tell me. Tell me what you need, honey. I'm here for *It's called* you." *THE BLOW JOB?*

Paul grabs her hand in both of his. It's the only move *TBD...* he uses on both Maggie and Alice in an otherwise re- *maybe* markable separation of how he treats the two women in *even* his life that he loves more than anything he could have *change* imagined. *title?*

"I wanna suck on you." → *great. feeling so many things RN. including*

Quiet. *confusion, which is perfect.*

Alice stares at Paul with eyes that carry not a hint of irony. Paul keeps looking, waiting for the irony. It does *this is* not come. *Let's*

"I want you in my mouth, Paul. I need it." *not sure landing. powwow* Paul continues the big-game irony hunting in her *& beat it* eyes. But there is nothing resembling that animal in there.

"Alice, I think that right now you're confus—"

"Paul, I need you to stop talking and do what I need."

"I don't think you're thinking strai—"

"Stop talking and give me what I need. I gotta feel it."

Paul lifts his left leg ever so slightly in anticipation of an impending exit from the sofa bed, and Alice reaches into Paul's lap and very quickly slips his penis through the hole of his plaid Target pajamas. It is an extremely erect if not altogether enormous penis.

"It's so little, Paul. Craig's was . . ."

Ha! Love this! Still confused & it's great

Paul is now completely frozen. He is too shocked to be offended. To even move. He is, as usual, fully in Alice's command.

"I'm gonna put it in my mouth. Just for a few seconds. Just to feel it. I gotta feel something else."

can we cut this? I'd rather not. "define it"

And without pause Alice slips Paul's penis into her mouth. And the tension in her body immediately releases. This Alice is suddenly no longer the bonky Alice of a few hours ago. She is fluid. She is relaxed. If her boyfriend of four years hadn't just been run over on Seventeenth Street by a recycling truck, one would guess from the movements in her shoulders and upper torso that she is truly happy.

Paul tries to speak, protest, anything. But his body takes over and all he can manage is a very quick and somewhat loud . . .

"Ohmigod. Uuuugh."

And just like that, it is over. Alice tucks Paul's penis back into his pajamas. She looks in his eyes with a relaxed, thankful stare.

"I'm sorry I made you do that. We don't have to tell Maggie. I'll never ask you to do anything like that again. I just really needed it. And I knew you of all people would understand. You're my best friend. I love you, Paul."

Paul blinks for the first time in three minutes.

"I love you too, Alice."

[handwritten: nice ending / unique & weird & true / love it]

Paul returns to his bedroom and lies down. This time
on his back. He does not close his eyes. He thinks about
Maggie. And Maggie's mass of curls. And about Alice.

[handwritten: crafty callback!]

And why he always feels compelled to do what she asks
of him. No matter what. This strange cosmic hold she
has on him. And Paul has a hard time figuring out what
this all means, especially in light of—

"Everything okay in there?"

[handwritten: nice "interruption" call back / u r killing it]

Paul looks over to see that Maggie is now awake,
watching him as he watches the ceiling.

"You were in there awhile. Everything all right?"

Paul turns to look at Maggie. All he wants to do is
stick his nose in those semi-dirty curls. The most comfortable place on the planet. But he is not sure that he
will ever get to do that again.

[handwritten note:]

OK. This story is super interesting. Tiny,
focused & humble. I know and like
all 3 characters. great work. here are
my big takeaways:

① Don't get too cute or try too hard w/
the language. When I feel you ~~trying~~
it bumps me. Lay back 20% with
the tricks (bonting, %, etc) and it'll be
right in the sweet spot.

② Think about the title. It's giving away your surprise which isn't great. But it's a catchy irreverent title that gets us interested from page 1 before the story picks up. Hm... let's discuss.

③ Biggest note = how am I supposed to feel about this blowjob? Sexy? Sad? Both? The answer might be that you don't want to control it. But I felt the ship get away from you here for better or worse. It feels like it's in a middle ground right now between you showing me how to feel or just letting ~~the reader~~ it be whatever the reader brings to it. I think you need to make a decision. My gut says lay back and let the reader project into it. Let's discuss.

Great work, Dupliss! I love it and we'll find it in 2-3 drafts
—J

From: mark duplass
To: jay duplass
Subject: BLOW|OB feedback

dupes. just wanted to say that I got your feedback on my BLOW|OB story and it was just fuckin awesome all around. not only was it helpful, but I guess I just wanna say that it made me acutely aware of how special our relationship is. that u handle me so well. that u are so thoughtful and gentle with the criticism. and, in general, that your honesty doesn't take the form of brutality.

whatever. blah blah. just wanna say I appreciate it and I kinda had a little moment reading it and it felt really special.

that's it.

love yous

dupiss face johnson

———————

From: jay duplass
To: mark duplass
Subject: RE: BLOW|OB feedback

hey dupes. thanks so much for this. kinda crazy that u sent it cuz I actually had a hard time sleeping last night after I sent that to you.

I've been wanting to bring something up with you and now is probably a terrible time cuz I don't wanna blow all the positive mojo we have going on this email chain but I also feel like I need to get something off my chest.

the truth is, I feel like I kinda held back on my feedback on your story. my instinct was, basically, "mark is trying something new and I want to be supportive and I don't want him to feel like I'm just crushing his soul so I'm gonna be gentler with the feedback."

but when I was going to sleep last night, jen and I were watching POSTCARDS FROM THE EDGE and I was watching how raw and real this mother and daughter were in the way they dealt with each other. and as brutal and toxic as their relationship was . . . I got weirdly jealous. cuz they could say anything to each other. and, at the end of the day, they know they love each other so it didn't matter. they didn't use kid gloves or anything.

so, what I really want to say is that I didn't love the blowjob story. I didn't really feel the importance of it and I just, kinda . . . I don't know. it didn't work for me. and I think rather than salvage it that you are too talented to waste time on something that just isn't really that interesting.

and I guess, on a bigger picture front, I'm saying that I feel like there is maybe a little bit of an . . . untruth or something in how we deal with each other sometimes? like we are so good at being positive and supportive and nurturing and loving that maybe we do it to a fault? and that it is a rhythm we have established since birth and almost a role people expect us to play so sometimes we just play it on autopilot? I don't know. I probably should have thought this through before emailing you, but . . . I guess that's the point. I don't wanna think things through perfectly anymore before we talk about things. I wonder if maybe we should let loose and fight and just . . . let it spill a bit more, u know?

it's late. I don't know if I should send this.

but I promised myself I would.

if this doesn't make sense and is offensive, I am deeply sorry. know that my love for you is unshakable and forever.

but still. I'm gonna send it. fuck. I'm nervous.

love yous too.

wilson sampras johnson, jr., esquire

_____

From: mark duplass
To: jay duplass
Subject: RE: BLOW|OB feedback

hey dupes. I hear this and am taking it in. in the spirit of trying to honor what you are looking for (rawness and a less considered, kid-glovey response), I definitely am feeling bummed and hurt and that u maybe could have said it in a nicer way.

gonna take a minute to ponder. I think I genuinely prefer communicating in a more respectful, held-back tone. but maybe it's just cuz I'm used to it. but I also know that I feel like shit right now, and it's mostly bc u didn't consider my feelings (as much as u normally do) in your last email.

maybe I'm just sensitive.

I don't know.

_____

From: jay duplass
To: mark duplass
Subject: RE: BLOWJOB feedback

fuck. that's the last thing I wanted to happen but now realize it was probably inevitable. and it's hard because I reread what I wrote and I want to stand by my point except for the fact that a) it hurt your feelings and b) you're not into communicating like this.

I feel like this is a case of us sharing the same fucking cable to our house but us wanting to watch different channels and I don't really know how to handle it.

maybe I'll take a beat and get back too.

for whatever it's worth, while I can't say with honesty that I'm sorry I said those things, I am TRULY sorry that they hurt you and I love you still and always.

and I think what killed me the most was that in every email I've gotten from u in the past twenty years u have done some weird sign-off fake name and you didn't even sign off at all on your last email.

ugh. that sucked. but I get it.

anyway, love u.

yours truly

h.i. mcdonough

———————

From: mark duplass
To: jay duplass
Subject: RE: BLOW|OB feedback

ok. feeling better and looking things over I see what u mean. we can be more real and somehow even closer if we take off the kid gloves and just . . . be truthful without so much decoration and care and delicacy.

I see that point.

and I think in the end my ego has always been a bit bigger than yours so it's gonna be a bit of a challenge for me.

so, how bout this?

I'll try to let things rip a bit more and maybe u can try to add one little layer of gentleness and see if we can meet in the middle?

_____

From: jay duplass
To: mark duplass
Subject: RE: BLOW|OB feedback

ha!

I am loving this. and, yes, I think this is a great plan.

thank u for considering it all and being so open to it.

that said, you still didn't sign off with one of your witty signatures and I know u did that on purpose to still make me feel like shit just a LITTLE bit longer for hurting your feelings (realizing how much power I am giving u in letting u know how important those sign-offs are to me and seriously regretting it).

yours in dignity and farts,

elmer dinglesplatt, c.p.a.

———————————

From: mark duplass
To: jay duplass
Subject: RE: BLOW|OB feedback

I have heard and accepted your response.

may our paths cross again one day.

best wishes for your continued success.

sincerely,

diarrhea party 2049

XII.

PEOPLE TALK A lot about the film business being an industry of feast or famine. This turned out to be true for us in 2006. After a year of trying to sell *The Puffy Chair,* we had finally closed our deal with Roadside Attractions and Netflix. Also, after a year of running around Los Angeles, taking general meetings, and trying and failing to sell TV show and movie pitches, we suddenly found ourselves getting hired for two studio jobs in rapid succession.

The first job was for a "blind deal" that we signed with Universal to write a script for them with the intention of directing it. They would pay us $100,000 to write a "yet to be determined" script. Which is how a blind deal works. Basically, we were to pitch them three ideas and they had to take one. If they didn't, they would pitch us three ideas and we had to take one. If we didn't, the deal would dissolve and we wouldn't get paid.

Luckily, they took our first pitch, a sports comedy about two brothers competing in their own personal twenty-five-event Olympics. This script would turn into *The Do-Deca-Pentathlon,* which with Universal's blessing we eventually made independently a few years later. It was a great process all around.

The second job turned out to be a real life-changer, an original idea that we concocted with our producer friend Michael Costigan. It was a film about a young man, overly attached to his single mother, who has trouble accepting his mom's new boyfriend into their lives. It was purposefully dark, funny, strange, and wild. It was called *Cyrus*.

We never thought a studio would go for this kind of film, but we sold our pitch in the room to our first choice and one of the best studios in town, Fox Searchlight. They were very popular at the time due to the success of films like *Juno, Sideways, The Savages, Little Miss Sunshine, Once*, and *The Wrestler*, among others. We felt that if we fit in anywhere inside the studio system, it would be with Searchlight. They were the leading force in what was becoming known as Indiewood . . . the perfect balance between independently minded storytelling and staying within the Hollywood system.

At first, the process was just like old times. Searchlight liked the idea well enough, and our producer was a friend who supported and trusted us creatively, so we were left on our own to write a draft of the script. Which we did. In our apartments like we always did. In roughly the same amount of time it took us to write *The Puffy Chair*. Three weeks or so.

When we handed in the script to the studio, we got our first glimpse into the new world we were entering. First off, they had never seen a script come in so fast. But truth be told, it took so long for our collective lawyers and agents to argue the contract points, we were actually done with the draft before our deal even closed. We waited for the legal ink to dry and ended up handing the script in the day the deal closed, about a month after we sold them the idea. This quick turnaround was utterly beyond them. But they were terrifically excited to read it.

Still, it took a little while for them to get around to it. And then a little more time to set the meeting where they would give us their feedback. And a little more time when they had to reschedule that meeting. To be clear, this timeline was fine for us because we were working on our other movie for Universal as well, but it was definitely surprising how long it took us to get that meeting after we turned the script in.

When we finally had that first official "script notes" meeting, it wasn't what we expected. Nor was it similar to the stock Hollywood lore of the executives being idiots who only wanted car chases, blood, and boobs. Our executives were incredibly intelligent, thoughtful individuals whose goal was to make the smartest, most interesting movie they could imagine. But it immediately struck us in the room that they believed, to their cores, they knew better than us. On almost all fronts . . . character, story, pace, tone, etc. And while they heaped praise on us for the things they said were "working" in this draft (by the way, it was never framed as their opinion but almost always as empirical fact), they were abundantly clear on the things that must change in order for the movie to "work."

Everything inside of us wanted to scream, "Yes, this is a different way to go with some of these choices, but is your way empirically better? Does your way work, and our way *not* work because it's different?" But we were still good Catholic school boys. And we had been to therapy, and we knew how to validate people's feelings and opinions, so we took in their notes and said we thought we could make a lot of these changes and would get back to them.

When we got home, we were pretty depressed. The changes weren't huge, but it was a bummer to be made to feel like they didn't respect us. That they felt that they just knew better. Still, it was a studio film—we knew we would have to make compromises—so we looked at their seven major notes and decided we could employ about four of those changes and still keep the DNA of the movie we wanted to make. We called them to let them know our thoughts, and they were respectful if not overjoyed that we weren't taking all of their changes to heart.

Over the next few weeks, we dug in on our rewrite. We stayed in the room together. Pacing. Emotionally eating chips and salsa and super-sugary cereals. And much of it was a struggle. We just felt that in the end we were trying to execute someone else's vision for our weird, dark, funny movie. And it was hard to swallow.

It took us a while to realize it, but we were slightly ashamed of the bastardization of our movie that we were allowing, and we didn't like doing it in front of each other. I remember Mark saying that it felt like masturbation . . . we know that we're both doing it, but at least we do it at home, alone, and don't have to witness each other doing it.

So we decided to divide and conquer on this one. The plan was that since we still had two movies to write (*Cyrus* and *The Do-Deca-Pentathlon*), we would work separately. I would take *Do-Deca* first and Mark would take *Cyrus* first. When we were done with a particular draft or rewrite, we would flip it to the other one to check the work and make it better. Then on the next draft we would switch. And we would "ping-pong" those drafts back and forth until the movies were done. It felt like a bit of a dirty secret, as both studios assumed they were getting both brothers to write at the same time, but ultimately we felt like trading drafts back and forth still gave it that same vibe. So we went for it. And interestingly enough, it went really well from a collaboration standpoint. It was actually an improvement all around, because what we didn't realize at the time was that we were beginning to work at very different paces. And this discrepancy was causing some conflict when we stayed in the same room together, hammering out the scripts line by line. Working alone allowed each of us to do it at our own pace in our own way.

But we still had the issue of trying to execute script notes that just weren't feeling right. Again, these were not horrid notes from stupid executives, but they were just not reflective of the kind of movie we thought we were making. And we began to feel burdened by the script-writing process. The best way to describe it is that it felt like a marriage that was on the rocks. We knew we loved each other, we knew the goal was worth it, but it was a lot of work and it was just really hard at times. So like members of a struggling marriage, we began to look outside of that marriage for inspiration and bliss. And this is where we learned about the "affair movie."

The affair movie is that movie you end up thinking about when you are supposed to be writing the one to which you are currently assigned. It's the easy, fun, "other" one that lingers in your mind while you are hammering away at an annoying detail of the writing assignment at hand. It beckons you like a Siren away from your "marriage movie." And the good news is, as opposed to actual infidelity, the affair movie can be quite productive and helpful while you are on assignment.

Our first affair movie was a story idea called *Baghead*. It was totally ridiculous. It was about four struggling actors who want to make the next great American indie film, so they retreat to a cabin with no skills and a ton of pump to write the script. The script in the film will be called *Baghead* and will be about someone with a paper bag over their head stalking them. And it's all fun and games until someone with a paper bag over their head *actually* begins stalking them. They don't know whether it's just one of them fucking with the group or there's a psycho out there.

At the time, this was the perfect antidote to the struggle of writing *Cyrus*. Not only was it a fun escape from the rigor of writing on assignment and pandering to notes we didn't fully agree with, but it also gave us something to focus on during the long, drawn-out process of waiting for the studio to read, respond, and set a notes meeting. It was so fun, and moved so quickly, that we had a final draft of *Baghead* done before we even got a response on the second draft of *Cyrus*. So, we thought, maybe *Baghead* would be our second film?

The production process of *Baghead* was its own interesting journey. Word had gotten out how cheaply we'd made *The Puffy Chair*, so film financiers were eager to pay for our next movie. However, we were not too excited to take $10,000 from someone and let them own all of our backend. In our minds, *Baghead* could be made comfortably for about $50,000. This would pay our crew pretty well, make a decent-looking film, and get us to a major festival to sell it for (hopefully) a decent profit. We thought if we could get about $250,000 from a financier to make *Baghead*, we'd give them a bunch of the backend, pay our crew even better, and walk away with a nice internal profit. Everybody wins!

As it turned out, almost everyone in town wanted to make *Baghead* for that price. We set up a week of meetings with financiers, who were all extremely excited to work with us. But what we were too naïve to realize was that they all had their conditions. They wanted to see exactly how the money was spent and have an accountant over our shoulders the whole time (aiming to reduce our budget and salaries as we went). Or they wanted to change the ending. Or they wanted way too much of the backend profit when we sold the film. What we wanted was simple:

> You liked *The Puffy Chair*. We made it our way. Give us $250,000 and we will deliver you a movie. But you have to let us do it our way. The good news is that you don't have to do anything!

But none of them could resist keeping their hands out of our cookie jar. So we thought long and hard about it and decided to take $50,000 of our writing fees and fund *Baghead* ourselves. It felt crazy—that we had worked so hard in the indie film scene for so long and we were *still* self-financing our movies—but it just seemed like the smartest and best way to protect how we made films. And in all honesty possibly the best financial move as well. We felt certain we could sell the movie for at least $100,000. It was a risk, but a calculated one, so we turned down all the financiers (who were shocked and offended) and decided to go make *Baghead* on our own, our way.

TOP 10 FILMS OF ALL TIME (PART 5)*

And, just like that, there were only eight films. Because we set aside one hour to finish the list. And promised each other that if we couldn't figure it out in one hour we would strike the list from the book altogether. So we each, unbeknownst to the other, came to the meeting prepared to make the ultimate sacrifice for the greater good of these stupid essays (and our brotherhood in general). We each knocked off not one but two films from our personal favorites.

And, just like that, the entire energy shifted. With two tiny acts of self-sacrifice, we had gone from the process of subtraction to addition. We had changed the energy in the room from compromise to collaboration. We smiled. And within the next six minutes we had our final list.

American Movie

Raising Arizona

Tootsie

Rocky

Hoop Dreams

The Crying Game (MD)

Dumb and Dumber

The Cruise (MD)

Henry Fool (JD)

The Horse Boy

You Can Count on Me

Close-Up (JD)

* *To be continued . . .*

WIVES

We sent the following questions in an email to our wives Jen Duplass (Jay) and Katie Aselton (Mark). They sent back the following responses. We haven't edited them.

Can you describe meeting the brother of your then-boyfriend/ now-husband and what your impression was of their relationship at the time?

JEN: When Jay and I were first dating, I noticed a CD in his car with "Merry Christmas Boopa Face" scrawled on the front in black Sharpie. I asked Jay what "Boopa Face" meant. He got really quiet, then he said, "I guess it literally means 'Shit Face'?" And I said, "Your brother calls you Shit Face?" And he said, "It's a . . . term of endearment?"

This was my first introduction to the Duplass brand of creativity, typically laced with levity and insular language.

When I first met Mark in person, he was sitting on the sofa watching TV. Our exchange was a brief hello. My first impression was that he was the type of person whose trust needed to be earned. After a few weeks, when he knew I was going to stick around, Mark warmed to me. I think things really took a turn after he and Jay made *This Is John*. When the guys were accepted into Sundance, I made them matching trophies. Extremely large trophies with functioning answering machines, spray-painted gold, for Best Actor and Best Director from the "Answering Machine Association of America," or something silly like that. After that, I felt that Mark really let me in and acted like the big brother I never had and always wanted (even though he is several years younger).

KATIE: I met Jay about six months into my relationship with Mark. Mark and I had just completed an epic road trip down the East Coast from Maine to Austin, so I was pretty delirious and don't remember many details. What I do remember is that Jay was training for a triathlon and was wearing full cycling apparel. He looked like he'd just stepped off the Tour de France. I also remember that, despite being dressed like Lance Armstrong, he was very sweet to me. As if he knew I wanted him to like me and he was going to make sure he gave me that impression.

As to their relationship at the time, because Mark and I were dating long-distance then, I had more of a secondhand understanding of their dynamic, as told to me by Mark. It was clear that Jay was the person Mark would turn to if we were having problems. Jay was who Mark would call after we fought. Jay seemed to be that best friend Mark turned to for guidance. They were more friends/brothers than business partners during this period, as Jay was running their editing business and Mark was off making music with his band Volcano, I'm Still Excited!! So I wasn't introduced to the complexities of their "shared creative brain" dynamic till later.

Was there ever a moment when you were taken aback by the nature of their dynamic and how they related to each other?

JEN: Early on, Jay told me that even though the guys had separate rooms as kids, they would almost always sneak into the same bed. His mom told me that they knew the boys were doing this but let them think they were getting away with something. Jay told me that they often stayed up late talking about their dreams until they fell asleep. I loved this. I never wanted to interfere with their special bond. I told Jay that if his brother didn't like me, I couldn't continue dating him.

KATIE: I was amazed how these two brothers shared every detail of themselves with each other. How emotionally evolved they were. How they were able to talk about all of their feelings . . . how creative . . . how supportive . . . really, just how much they loved each other. Until you see it personified, you don't realize how rare it is. But they were also still dude-like with each other in many ways—these uber-sensitive guys who were as obsessed with feelings as they were with burps and farts. Usually those interests don't go together. Their equal love of therapy and *Dumb and Dumber* struck me as wonderfully weird and interesting.

Some people talk about how, through the years, they have had difficulty being around "The Brothers." How sometimes they can be a bit insular or even exclusive. Have you ever felt this way?

JEN: I think their creative marriage is just as important as Jay's and mine. Maybe it's because I'm an introvert and a bit of a voyeur, but I find the balancing act of their work relationship and brotherhood fascinating. I have two sisters that I love, and I can't imagine the pressure that a creative marriage would add to my relationships with them. Also, I don't have to work with the brothers like Katie does!

KATIE: I could probably write a whole book on the love triangle that was the making of *The Puffy Chair*. Mark and I were two years into our relationship, starring in a movie together about a couple who ultimately break up, written and directed by Jay and Mark. It was a beautiful experience and also an extremely difficult one. For instance, it was a collaborative process. Until it wasn't. And one or more of us would get our feelings hurt. And then it would be collaborative again. Sometimes I'd be in on the core creative conversations, and then Mark and Jay would up and go on a two-hour walk without me and come back with a whole new game plan. There were times we were all together as a team. Then it was me against Mark and Jay, them against me, me and Jay against Mark, me and Mark against Jay. It was quite the odd triangle there for a bit. I think I struggled because, ultimately, Jay and Mark's creative partnership won out (as it should have) and I felt threatened by that at times. In the end we made a movie that we are all really proud of, so I sometimes wish I could go back and do it all over again as a more mature, emotionally evolved human who understands their dynamic more. That said, I really believe that some of that turmoil fed into the energy of the movie . . . and I love that.

Anything else?

JEN: Not many people know this, but Jay and Mark's secret weapon is their dad, Larry. He's a trial lawyer and mediator and is integral to helping the guys through times when they get gridlocked. Their mom, Cindy, is also on board to love them up unconditionally and add levity with her endless nicknaming. The four of them are a fine-tuned little ecosystem. Not to minimize our roles as wives; this is just my take on the four original Boopa Faces and the magic that makes them who they are.

KATIE: There are many nicknames in the Duplass family. It's a symbol of the unbridled creativity and goofiness that runs rampant in our family. I myself have more than ten ridiculous nicknames (including "Kruge," which is short for Freddy Krueger). Everyone calls everyone by whatever nickname they prefer on a given day. Except for "Dupes." This is what Jay and Mark call each other. It seems to be reserved just for them. I love that they still have an exclusive nickname for each other. Even though they are in their forties.

IN DEFENSE OF AIR SUPPLY

IF YOU LOOK up the most commonly used adjective to describe Air Supply's "All Out of Love," I believe you would get *cheesy*. Maybe *over the top*. Maybe *melodramatic*. Hard to argue with those. But there's a secret to Air Supply. Depending on the emotional state in which you find yourself, this fuzzy-haired overly sensitive band can be . . . the greatest band of all time. It can be everything you've ever needed. You just have to know when to seek out Air Supply and when to stay away.

For instance, some days you are at the top of your game. You're feeling confident. Your brain is vital, inspired, and alert. Your energy is up. You are firing on all cylinders. These are the days when you want to musically challenge yourself with one of the obtuse string quartets from Bartók. Or the twelve-tone compositions of Shostakovich. Go on. Get in there. Get artsy-fartsy. See what you can swallow. Try to make your way through that dense, extremely challenging art into the space of the feels. It's hard work, but worth it if you can break through. You'll be proud of yourself.

But what if you're having a different day? What if you are feeling particularly vulnerable on an early winter morning, snuggled under a blanket? Or even better . . . you have the flu and are somewhat dizzy with fever. Do you really want to dig through the B sides of early Brian Eno? I don't think so. This is the time for Air Supply. Open your arms to their high-pitched falsettos. Embrace their on-the-nose lyrics and lushly overdramatic three-part harmonies. And when the final repeated chorus adds the string section and swells toward that glorious climax, it will make you feel more deeply and profoundly than any restrained, intelligent piece of music will ever have the chance to make you feel.

We bring this up because it keeps occurring to us how arbitrary our reception of art is these days. We keep saying things like "That's a good film" or "What a terrible painting," when in reality our own subjective experience of that thing is really what we're talking about. And we're not just talking about the differences in people's empirical tastes. We're saying that our very *own* taste is actually completely subjective and can change on a given day. A good example of this is when one of us went to the movie theater to see a Hollywood film by the name of *Titanic*. Let's just call this person Jark to avoid any specific embarrassment. At the time Jark Duplass was already a refined film student and fan of Tarkovsky, Godard, and Cassavetes. He could discern and write cogent essays on the nuances and subtleties of the various eras of cinematic history. But today, Jark was having some relationship troubles and was about to go on a big trip by himself. And Jark was feeling a bit . . . vulnerable. When Jark saw a bit of himself in a young Leo DiCaprio, he proceeded to cry his balls off for three hours straight in that movie theater.

Jark knew then and knows now that *Titanic* is not the greatest movie of all time. But there is no denying that Jark had one of his peak emotional cinematic experiences at the hands of James Cameron. And there's no taking that back. Is it his fa-

vorite film? No. Is it his favorite viewing experience? Well . . .
it's close.

So we've begun to curate lists for what types of art we
should take in depending on our mood. We'll often see a
trailer for a film and designate its viewing for "the next time I
get strep throat" (*The Blind Side*). Cuz Jark now knows that, in
his normal semi-cynical pseudo-intellectual state, he might
scoff at some of the manipulative cinematic maneuverings of
a melodramatic sports drama. But once that thermometer
hits one hundred degrees, all bets are off.

So instead of making fun of Air Supply or films like *The
Notebook* and *The Bridges of Madison County*, break out one of
those suckers on a day when you are feeling "less than" and
they just might take you on the very emotional adventure
you've been waiting for.

AIRPORT

#3

(In Chicago's O'Hare Airport, Terminal 3, there is a particularly delicious-looking fast food Chinese stall in the mini food court. We are trying to resist its seductive tractor beam. We should be going to Jamba Juice instead, ordering something with less MSG, fat, and salt. But when we are on a promotional tour, talking about ourselves and our "art" for up to twelve hours at a stretch, we develop a particularly low opinion of ourselves. And the Chinese food seems not only comforting and delicious but something that we somehow deserve . . . as reward and punishment.

But then Mark sees something that catches his attention. Two older ladies, likely in their seventies, are eating lunch together in the food court. They are smiling, talking. This feels like the beginning of a vacation for them. Mark pokes me in the ribs to get my attention. The one on the right wears a long-sleeved plain T-shirt and a pair of jeans. She dresses more like a woman half her age. But she looks a bit older than the woman on the left, who wears a matching two-piece casual suit from a place like Ann Taylor LOFT. In this way, these two women are different. But their mannerisms, their smiles, their rhythms with each other, all suggest that they are very close.)

JAY: (*pointing to the one on the right with the T-shirt and jeans*)
Alice.
MARK: (*pointing to the one on the left in the matching two-piece*)
Jean.

(*We sit on the names for a bit. They work.*)

MARK: Heading to Florida?

(*It's winter. A logical destination. But something doesn't feel
right about it.*)

JAY: Palm Springs.
MARK: Yes. Palm Springs.
JAY: Warm.
MARK: A place where people can get a fresh start.
JAY: Uh-huh.

(*We consider what comes next. Suddenly Mark puts his hand
on my knee. This means something has come to him in what
we call a "flop"—i.e., the idea is nearly fully formed.*)

MARK: Alice's husband passed away last year. She's had a hard
time. She's dressing like their daughter now, jeans and T-
shirts, trying to find out who she is and who she wants to be.
She read an article in *The New Yorker* about how older women
who lose their husbands often enter lesbian relationships.
The comfort and understanding is there among women, and
as they approach the end of life . . . you know, that kind of
comfort becomes more important than the previously crucial
element of sexual attraction when looking for a mate. She
hasn't told Jean this, but she had an affair with one of the local

female librarians. To kind of try things out. It made her realize two things. One, she can enjoy sex with a woman. Two, the next woman she wants to have sex with is Jean.

(I smile. This is pretty good. And we both watch the two ladies as they giggle and enjoy each other's company. The thought of them finding love at a late age is terrifically exciting to both of us.)

MARK: But Jean is married. Not a great marriage, which she is the first one to admit. But still, it's a vow. And Alice is nervous as to how to broach the idea of the two of them being together. Spending their last years laughing and traveling and enjoying life off the life insurance money she has just received.

(Mark spends himself here. And looks to me with a nod that I can jump in now. That Mark has hit the wall and needs me. I like being needed.)

JAY: So Alice has booked a trip for them to Palm Springs. A predominantly gay male community. The liberal sexuality will surround them, potentially setting the stage for this conversation Alice so desperately wants to have with Jean.
MARK: But she's terrified.
JAY: Fucking terrified! Jean is her best friend! What if she offends Jean? Scares her off? Or, even worse, Jean politely says no and things are forever changed between them with the knowledge that Alice is harboring more than platonic feelings toward her.

(We look at the smiling face of Alice. It takes on a new light. As if we can feel the tension and the fear of how much she

wants things to work out with Jean. And that the laughter is just a game. Interesting how our projections, which are no doubt utterly false, can change the way we perceive her.)

MARK: But in the end Alice has to go for it. She has to follow her heart.
JAY: For what is life if a life is half-lived?
MARK: Good one.
JAY: Little over the top?
MARK: Kinda, but it totally worked. This is big stuff. Love. Friendship. End-of-life stuff.

(We both nod. Feeling it. Loving these two women and what they will be going through in the next few days. This game is so fun. We could play it forever. And probably will. Then we take a breath. Our story seems to be done, at least for now.)

MARK: I don't think I can do the Chinese food. I just don't want that in my body while I'm stuck on a plane.
JAY: Agreed. Jamba?
MARK: Jamba.

(Cut to: Ten minutes later. We are in the Jamba Juice line and I am having a thought. When I have these kinds of thoughts, usually my face changes. Mark notices immediately and checks in with me.)

MARK: Whatcha got?
JAY: I'm having another thought.

(Mark knows what this means. While he is really good at getting those stories on their feet in his "flop," I am usually

*the one tasked to make that story more unique and nuanced
upon further introspection. I'm the one who saves us from
the somewhat mediocre first draft of a story. I am supposed
to take it to a deeper level. It's a lot of pressure. Mark knows
this and genuinely appreciates it.)*

JAY: What if *Jean* was the one who read the *New Yorker* article
about women entering lesbian relationships later in life?
And when reading it, she couldn't help but think that Alice
was in that very situation. Recently widowed, liberal sensi-
bilities, even hanging around that librarian a little bit lately.
And Jean, who is a classic overthinker, started to wonder . . .
"Oh no! Is Alice angling to turn our relationship into something more than platonic? Did she ask me on this trip to . . .
pitch me on it? I mean, we're headed to Palm Springs, for
Chrissake!"

(This makes us laugh. Always a great sign.)

MARK: Meanwhile—and I think this is where you're headed—
Alice actually has no such intentions with Jean.
JAY: Absolutely not.
MARK: She just wanted a fun girls' trip to cheer her up around
the anniversary of her husband's death. ·
JAY: Yep. But because Jean is paranoid, every time Alice puts
her arm around her or fixes her hair for her—even offers to
share an entrée—Jean tenses up and closes off to Alice . . .
MARK: . . . who can't help but wonder, "Why is Jean being so
weird with me?" This is soooo good.
JAY: It all culminates in a big fight at the craft fair. Jean ulti-
mately apologizes for projecting that shit onto Alice, and
Alice is able to laugh it off because they are old friends who

have been through so much. And things return back to nor-mal.

(*Here, I let it sit. I'm done. And I must admit, I did a good job rebooting this idea.*)

MARK: But they don't fully return to normal.

(*And now Mark has a new idea. This is our collaboration at its best. Building on each other's ideas. Improving them. And having fun.*)

MARK: Because the well has been poisoned. The fact re-mains . . . Jean's marriage is not healthy. And Alice *is* looking for a partner, though she doesn't know where to begin. So Jean shows her the *New Yorker* article . . . so they can have a good laugh about it.
JAY: Which they do.
MARK: And they have a big, fun, fancy dinner to celebrate getting over that weird moment.
JAY: Lots of rosé.
MARK: Tons.
JAY: And they go for a drunken swim back at the hotel.
MARK: And order room-service french fries and more wine back in Jean's room.
JAY: And watch something kinda dumb and romcom-y on pay-per-view.
MARK: And feel adorably "naughty" because of all the bad language.
JAY: And stay up late talking about how much fun they're hav-ing. And how Alice has all this money now and they should

travel more together. Enjoy their lives. There's not much time left.

MARK: And they find themselves practically quoting that *New Yorker* article.

JAY: And then it just gets quiet. And each thinks how wonderful it is that they can have a raging party together but also just sit in silence too. How rare that connection is.

MARK: And they just smile at each other as the air in the room starts to shift.

(We nod at each other, waiting to see who is going to be the one to make them kiss. Who has the best idea for how it should go down. We smile at each other, sucking on Jamba Juice, waiting for the idea to come. We are way too pleased with ourselves and our stupid little airport game. And we're oddly fine with that.)

XIII.

SHOOTING *BAGHEAD* WAS a fucking blast. A cast and crew of about ten of us all went down to Austin for three weeks of hell, but the best kind of hell. We were up all night, running around in the middle of the woods like idiots. We were making up ways to do stunts that ended up looking amazing. Everyone was doing every possible job: Jay shot the main camera, I held the boom pole, we all (including the actors) hung lights in between scenes, and we all lived and cooked together. We would discuss ways to improve scenes moments before shooting them. We'd throw out the script and improvise when we were inspired. Most important, with no one to answer to or explain ourselves to, we followed our own impulses the whole way. We came away exhausted but oddly invigorated and inspired in a way we hadn't felt since shooting *The Puffy Chair* two years earlier.

On the studio front, we held up our end of the development bargain with *Cyrus* and Fox Searchlight during this time. We developed a sense of compromise through the script note process that neither party was unhappy with, if not altogether excited by. And the project moved forward toward our mutual goal of us directing the movie once Searchlight was happy with the script. In short, we were a marriage in peril, but we were in therapy and hoping to work it out.

There was some good news on that front. We sent an early draft of the *Cyrus* script to our friend Jonah Hill, who happened to be a big fan of *The Puffy Chair,* and he really flipped for the lead character of Cyrus and agreed to play the role. From there we scored John C. Reilly, Marisa Tomei, and Catherine Keener as our other three leads. So in terms of casting, we had a dream scenario. We just needed Searchlight to be happy enough with our script to greenlight the movie. Which, as you might imagine, was a long and somewhat painstaking process. To be clear, we understood why they were nervous. We hadn't made a movie for more than $50,000, and the budget for *Cyrus* was coming in just under $7 million. They wanted to secure their investment, make the script as airtight as possible before committing all that cash. But the drawn-out script notes were wearing us down, and we were losing our inspiration for *Cyrus* over the course of the lengthy, microcosmic development process.

Back on the indie scene (why does this suddenly feel like sports reporting?) we had just gotten word that Sundance had accepted *Baghead*. The programmers loved it, and (as opposed to *The Puffy Chair*) we were being given a prime-time screening slot in a more prestigious division. The movie was not perfect (we did make it quickly and with reckless abandon), but it was inspired and people were responding to its freshness. When we showed up for our premiere, the theater was not only packed but every buyer was there in full force. It seemed that the air around this film was different, ready for explosion, but we had also experienced the lull of *The Puffy Chair* taking an entire year to sell, so we didn't want to get our hopes up.

As we watched *Baghead* play at its premiere, we felt great. When we got up afterward for the Q&A session, we saw some film buyers we recognized scurrying out of the theater on their cellphones. We locked eyes at the back of the room with Josh Braun, our sales agent and dear friend and collaborator, who gave us a wry thumbs-up. Even though we were both suffering from a mild flu, we were secretly hoping that this would be our first experience with the famed Sundance bidding war.

For those of you unfamiliar with the film festival environment and Sundance in particular, there is something kind of insane that happens during these January weeks up in the mountains. People are altitude-sick, excited, rushed, and panicked they will miss out on a film sale. And when a great movie pops up, it will sometimes go all night and into the wee hours of the morning with different studios and buyers vying back and forth with the sales agent. So when we came out of the theater that night and Josh said, "Get in the car, it's going to be a long night," we were snotty and feverish but ridiculously excited.

Our first meeting was with a medium-size buyer who had already put in a lowball bid to try to buy the movie before anyone else. And they put a timer on it to pressure us to take it before they could be outbid by a bigger company. It was already worth more than we paid to make the movie, so we were instantly relieved that we would at least not lose money on the film. We were, as our dad always said, playing with the bank's money at this point.

Right before we entered the condo, Josh pulled us aside and handed us a cellphone.

"What's this?"

He told us that about ten minutes into the meeting that cellphone would ring. We were to look at the phone, look at each other, and excuse ourselves from the meeting and thank them for their interest.

"Why?"

Josh smiled the knowing smile of James Bond. It was a smile that said, "Let the games begin." We couldn't have been more excited. And, sure enough, right in the middle of the meeting our phone rang. We did our best (likely terrible) acting job and quickly scurried out of the meeting.

Oddly enough, it wasn't a bluff. We actually did have another meeting set up. We were going to rendezvous with an intern for a large studio (which shall remain anonymous) who was waiting for us, in his pajamas, in the parking lot of the movie theater where we screened. It was now about one A.M., and we were dropping off a film print to him so that he could drive it all night from Park City to Los Angeles and show his boss the film first thing in the morning.

I mean . . . come on. Seriously? This just kept getting better. The only problem was, we were now feeling guilty because we hadn't yet shown up to the after-party for our own film. But Josh informed us that we were not allowed to go to that party. Because film buyers might be there, and if they saw us there they might feel that we weren't directly engaged in the sale of the movie, and we wanted everyone thinking that we were in a condo somewhere meeting with another buyer. To drive that Sundance bidding frenzy if possible.

We took another meeting with a big distributor, and it was clear within a few minutes that they didn't want to buy the film but only wanted to get face time with us and pitch us on some other movie they were making. After that disappointment, we got a call that one of our favorite distributors was interested. Their junior person and one of the partners had seen it and loved it, but the other main partner was sick in bed with the flu (probably the same one we had) and had not made it out to see the film. He was currently in bed watching it on a DVD screener that our sales agent had delivered to him an hour before. And while he was only halfway through, he knew that he liked it enough to meet with us and discuss the film.

So at about 2:45 A.M., we headed over to his condo deep in the snowy woods of Park City and took a meeting with one of Hollywood's most elite film executives while he was still in his pajamas. It was not unlike the climactic drug deal scene from *Boogie Nights*, except that Night Ranger wasn't playing in the background and we were all doing peppermint tea instead of cocaine. And it ended much more harmoniously.

He loved the movie. We all liked one another. They were going to send us an offer within the hour.

Exhausted and fully adrenaline-crashed, we headed back to our cheap little condo. It was about four A.M. We found the only place open and ordered a pizza and some beer. We paid way too much for it while we waited in a daze for the phone to ring.

At four-thirty we got the call. Sony Pictures Classics, which had put out some of our all-time favorite movies, was offering us almost half a million dollars to buy the U.S. rights to our tiny movie *Baghead*. But they wanted us to answer right away. We couldn't wait for the other big studio to see our film print the next morning via the pajama'd intern driving all night in the snow back to Los Angeles. We were not allowed to wait for the next screening where someone might outbid them.

We looked at each other and knew instantly that we would take the deal. That we had gambled on ourselves and won. That we had somehow managed to make this movie exactly how we wanted to make it, and we had made much more money for ourselves and our cast and crew than if we had done it with traditional studio financing.

We thanked Josh, who we still work with today, and hung up the phone. Our pizza and beer came and we had a little of it, but not a ton because we were utterly wiped out. But before we went to bed that night (oddly enough, in twin beds in the same room, although not in the same bed, that would just be weird), there was one more conversation to be had.

MARK: Dupiss?
JAY: Yeah, Dupes.

(*Pause.*)

MARK: What are we gonna do about *Cyrus*?
JAY: Was just thinking about that . . . I don't know.
MARK: Cuz . . . that movie is feeling hard. And I'm having this feeling that it's not gonna get any better than making movies with you, the way we always have. On our own.
JAY: Me too.

(*Pause.*)

MARK: Fuck.
JAY: Yeah. Fuck.

TRUE BELIEVER

In December 1981, I was five years old and I was rummaging through a dense closet in the guest room when I found a stack of presents. They were wrapped in green and red paper. By this age Jay had already taught me how to read, so I could make out the labels.

TO: MARK
FROM: SANTA

It was a bit of a dizzying moment for me. I tried to do the basic math. Yep, it was still early in December, so it wasn't Christmas morning yet. Were these left over from last year? That seemed unlikely, and even if that was true, why would the presents be buried behind all of my parents' summer clothes instead of under the tree where Santa normally put them?

I did what I always did in situations like this. I went to get my big brother and ask him what was happening. I was able to drag Jay away from his Erector set for a moment to show him my confusing discovery. I didn't get to see his face the moment he saw the presents because I was behind him, but I remember feeling his body go rigid. He stayed very still. And he very specifically didn't look at me. He simply said, "I'll be right back," and left me standing there. I was little (and dumb) so I just waited there for what must have been at least ten minutes. Then Jay came back and sat me down for a talk.

What I didn't know then was that Jay used his ten minutes to speak with my parents. Not being privy to the actual convo, legend has it that it went something like this:

JAY: Guys, Mark found the Santa presents in the closet.
MOM: Oh no.
JAY: I told you guys you should have hidden them better.
DAD: What did you say to him?
JAY: I didn't say anything, I just came to talk to you guys.

(*Head shaking and regret from some guilty parents. Then . . .*)

JAY: Let me go talk to him.
Mom: We should be the ones to tell him.
JAY: Hold on. Don't do that yet. He's only five. He's not that smart. He's kinda dumb, actually. I think I can work on him.

(*NOTE: Through the years there have been a lot of conversations like this. Me being a bit of a wild card that needs managing, my parents befuddled as to how to deal with me, and Jay being the level-headed negotiator that kept the Duplass household on track. A little bit like Tom Hagen in* The Godfather.)

When Jay sat me down, he carefully explained to me that when he was five years old he also found presents in the closet and got confused. He told me that he went to Mom and Dad and they explained the whole situation. That, if you really think about it, Santa has so much work to do on the actual Christmas Eve that he couldn't possibly deliver all the presents that very night. So he enlists the help of parents all around the world to do some early delivery of presents to lighten his load on the actual day. And we were one of the lucky families Santa had chosen for a predelivery of sorts. Mom and Dad hide the presents ahead of time in early December and then place them under the tree on Christmas Day. And that's how it works.

Jay leaned back, smiled, and peered into my eyes for signs of disbelief. I remember a weird tingling feeling inside. My bullshit detector was going off. But at the same time, the person I loved and trusted most in this world was looking at me with loving eyes and talking to me. Plus, let's be honest, I really wanted to believe in Santa Claus. Still, I was skeptical.

So, for the next week, Jay ran an exhaustive campaign to reconvince me that Santa was real. It included geography lessons about the world's truly dizzying size. Census information from our burgundy Encyclopedia Britannica set about the sheer magnitude of the world's population. And then some very basic math about how fast Santa would have to travel to get it all done in one night. I wasn't smart, but I was old enough to understand that Santa dropping *all* those presents in one night to every kid in the world was an impossible task. So I decided to drink Jay's Santa Kool-Aid and buy back in.

And for the next two years I was a true believer in Santa. Until some dickhead kid on the bus bragged about there being no Santa and ruined it all again. But before that, Jay bought me two more magical Christmas seasons believing in Santa because he knew me well enough and cared about me enough to make it happen.

INVESTING

OKAY. WE DON'T really know anything about this stuff. But we somehow made a really good chunk of money buying some young, cheap stocks (with very little savings) that eventually skyrocketed. We recommend that you try to do the same. Set aside a month where you don't go out to eat. Use that savings to invest in a stock that you think has upside. Which stock? Good question. It's hard to figure out which stocks to buy. We've taken an approach that is fairly simple but works well. We only buy stocks of companies that we use, love, and believe in. We also limit it to stocks of which we have fairly intimate knowledge. For instance, we read the film industry trades every day. We know which companies have the best employees, best success rates, good reputations, etc. We feel we are in a unique position to know which media companies have a better chance at succeeding than others.

An example. In 2002 we were renting DVDs from a new mail order business called Netflix. Their customer service was great, it was cheap, everyone we showed the company to loved it and kept talking about it, so we bought a slew of shares in 2005 when they were only $20 apiece. Now, they are worth about fifty times that. Of course, we wish we had bought a lot more, but that purchase single-handedly funded one of our smaller films with its profits.

So look around in your life for that small company that no one really knows a lot about but you believe could be big. Get in early.

XIV.

AFTER WE SOLD *Baghead* to Sony Pictures Classics at Sundance, there was a definite shift for us back in L.A. The noise about our sale and how we made the movie spread quickly through the industry. We began getting offers to direct movies that were already greenlit. Not great movies or great offers, but offers nonetheless. One of the financiers (the one who had asked us to change the ending of *Baghead* as a condition to funding the film) sent us a particularly telling email that said, simply: "Crow not so tasty."

In short, companies were coming around to seeing how our way of doing things had its value. And one of these companies was Fox Searchlight, which called to congratulate us on our *Baghead* sale. On this same call, because this is the irony of how the world seems to work, they officially greenlit *Cyrus* to production. It was, technically speaking, a filmmaker's dream come true. A major studio was greenlighting our movie! They were going to give us millions of dollars to direct our movie!

But it wasn't that simple. Not only were we just beginning to realize that we could make movies on our own dime in the exact way we wanted to make them, but the sale of *Baghead* had proven that those little indie movies could be just as lucrative if not more so than some studio paychecks.

But we had put all this work into *Cyrus* and we still very much loved that story. So we promised to clear our calendars the next day and take a slow, thoughtful, objective read of the current *Cyrus* script and talk about it afterward. It was a while before I called Mark or he called me. Certainly longer than the ninety minutes it normally takes to read a script.

When we finally connected, we didn't have to say a thing. We both felt the same way. After all the rewriting and back and forth with the studio over the past year, we hardly recognized our little movie anymore. A screenwriter much more experienced than us once described the development process as a series of small steps away from your home. You build a home, then the studio starts asking you to take tiny little steps away. So you do. They are just tiny steps. But at a certain point, you look up to get your bearings and you discover that you are not only down the street, you've taken a few turns as well along the way, and you can't even see your fucking house anymore.

And that's exactly how we felt with *Cyrus*. But we are not irrational divas or fussy auteurs. We are practical, and we wanted to find a way to make the movie work. So after much discussion among ourselves and our incredibly patient producer, Michael Costigan, we decided we would tell Fox Searchlight that we only wanted to make the movie if we could go back to a much earlier draft of the script. One that represented a decent compromise of our original vision and a few of the key notes that they felt strongly about. Again, we have been to therapy, we know about compromise and intensely difficult collaboration because of our own complex relationship, so this solution seemed like a fair one.

When we presented it to the studio, we could tell that they weren't happy, but we also had the actors' support in this cause, and this is when we realized how powerful actors are in this business. Most likely, Searchlight agreed to our request in order to get the movie rolling and to keep the actors (who were paid well below their quotes in order to work with us) happy. *Cyrus* was greenlit and we just hoped and prayed that the studio would be a bit more laid-back during production than they were during the writing process.

At the same time, there was a whole other challenge that we faced in the making of *Cyrus*. We hadn't made a movie with a cast and crew of more than ten people since *Vince Del Rio*—the biggest piece of shit we'd ever created. Yay! Needless to say, we were a bit afraid of opening up our tiny, family-friendly creative process to an entire union crew of more than a hundred people. Our whole filmmaking philosophy was built on keeping things small and intimate on set so that we could focus on the two core tenets of our ethos: Get good performances and tell a good story.

Luckily, we hired the greatest assistant director in the world in the form of Cas Donovan. Cas was a fan of our little movies, had worked on huge movies, and vowed to guide us and protect us through our first big-budget movie experience. Which she did. As much as she possibly could. But there were times when the machine of a big movie would get in the way.

For instance, the first take we did of the film was a rather intimate scene between John Reilly and Catherine Keener. When we yelled cut, it was like a tornado hit the house. Crew members rushed in from every possible entrance, fixing hair and makeup, resetting props, adjusting lighting, tweaking lavalier microphones. And while they happened to be awesome people doing their jobs very well, as far as we were concerned they had obliterated any ounce of genuine intimacy we had built. So that night we had a meeting and discussed a new way of working.

The next day we told our crew that we would be treating every scene as if it were a nude scene: Only the essential people needed to film would be allowed on set. Everyone else would watch from a monitor outside. And when we yelled cut, no one was allowed to come into the set until the scene was done (unless it was an emergency of some sort). This process helped us maintain the intimacy and feel of our smaller films. And the actors really seemed to love it. In particular, we could tell they enjoyed that our attention was focused solely on them and not the more technical elements that often suck up directors' time and energy.

After a few days, things seemed to be dialing in. Our studio was watching all of our daily footage and had some comments here and there, but they were small things, so we just proceeded and assumed everything was fine. Around day four, things changed.

We got word that some of the executives wanted to come by the set to speak with us about some "concerns." We asked if it could wait. After all, it was a long shooting day and we wanted to get some sleep and see our families for a bit. But they insisted that it was important. So after we shot for thirteen hours, a van pulled up outside of set and we were ushered inside to have a conversation with our executives. And the crucial element that could not wait to be discussed was . . . throw pillows.

Yes. Throw pillows.

It seemed there was a growing concern that the beginning of the movie looked a bit too "brown" and "down" in our lead character's apartment. Now, to be clear, these executives were likely carrying the message from one of their bosses who saw some dailies and thought the movie looked "depressing." One of their bosses who knew that the people who came to see Fox Searchlight movies were women over the age of thirty-five, and those women liked things to look nice. So maybe some throw pillows would help liven things up a bit! And we understood this line of thinking. But it was a particularly hard pill to swallow at this moment. Ushered into a van like criminals, after an all-day shoot, being asked to reshoot a scene because it needed more throw pillows. All we could think was "But this character is a depressed divorcé with no money . . . his apartment is supposed to be brown. *And* down. He wouldn't have fucking throw pillows."

The thing is, Mark didn't just think this. He said it. Loudly. In fact, he pretty much screamed it. And then something very interesting happened. They were all taken aback. I came right in, and while I didn't yell, I reinforced Mark's point. More emphatically than we had ever done before. And we told them why they were wrong about that choice. And why we decided to dress his apartment that way. And how that was the way it should be. And that we didn't want to reshoot the scene. And then we told them we needed to get some sleep so we could be fresh for tomorrow's thirteen-hour shoot. And we left the van without being polite or validating. We buried the good Catholic boys inside of us right there and went home. And from that moment forward, they pretty much let us do our thing. Which was a wonderful and terrible thing in the end.

It was great because we, to this day, are endlessly proud of that movie. But it also meant that during the entire development process, when we were trying to listen, trying to compromise, trying to validate the thoughts of our executive collaborators, we were somehow perceived as either being weak or, even worse, lacking in clear vision. And the moment we started yelling was the moment they started backing away and allowing us to do more of what we wanted.

In the end, our collaboration with Fox Searchlight on *Cyrus* was (on the whole) a successful one. We got to make the movie we wanted to make. They were happy with it. It was well reviewed and made them a few million dollars of profit. As to our creative conflicts at the time, we get that we were likely a bit too young and naïve to truly understand what a studio movie required of us, and they get that maybe they could have been a bit more trusting that we knew what we were doing (we are actually all friends and laugh about it now).

But the one thing that sticks with us still is our fear that this industry (whether it's aware of this or not) doesn't actually reward the tenets of validation, listening, and hugs. That instead it rewards that baseball-cap-wearing, gum-chewing, cocky young director who yells at people to get what he wants. That somehow the disgusting behavior of fear, intimidation, and yelling is an expression of a filmmaker's "vision" and one that merits support.

And we talk about this phenomenon all the time. About how we always imagined we would have one foot in the indie world and one foot in the studio world. And how one of those two feet kinda feels a little rotten and soul-sick sometimes. And how it has affected the way we make movies today in a significant way.

THE BOX

WHEN MARK AND I were little, we started a slew of businesses together. Mostly they involved a lot of theorizing of how we would dominate the world through a certain product and its inevitable financial windfall, and then the idea would fizzle before we could actually make anything. And the reason for the fizzling was often due to Mark's lack of attention span or inability to enact our plan because he was four years my junior.

This is when our friend Brandt entered the picture. He lived across the street from us and was in the grade below me. In general, he played extremely well with me and Mark (he was and continues to be one of the nicest and purest souls on the planet), but every now and then there were things Brandt and I wanted to do that Mark was simply not old enough to do. We tried to be nice about it. We never threw it in his face that we were going to ride our bikes to the mall without him. But I could tell it burned him a little bit here and there.

One weekend, however, Brandt and I concocted a business plan of our own. I can't remember anything about the actual business except that we were terrifically excited about the name:

J&B, INCORPORATED.

Jay and Brandt. J&B. Its genius, as far as we were concerned, was in its simplicity. And also the fact that there was an existing logo we could co-opt from the brand of cheap Scotch. So we went to an empty lot in our neighborhood, "borrowed" wood scraps from the abandoned construction, and set about making some sort of box that would serve our business. Exactly how it would serve us I have no recollection, but we just wanted to build some shit, so that's what we did. I don't really remember what Mark was up to at the time, but this was the kind of summer day we'd normally spend together. He was just gone and on his own trip somewhere as far as I was concerned.

When we finished assembling the box, we spray-painted our "J&B" logo on it and stepped back to examine our creation. It was lopsided, unstable, and really stupid-looking. We were pretty proud of ourselves.

At dinner that night, I remember my mom pulling me aside and asking me if I would be willing to include Mark in the new business venture. And I remember it really made me upset that she asked. Being only nine years old, I couldn't identify why it bothered me, but I think I understood deep down that I was a very good big brother who almost always included Mark, and I wanted a pass on this particular project. And I was upset that my mom didn't see that and offer me that pass. I can't remember what I said, but I remember bucking her on it. Saying something about the fact that it was Brandt's and my idea and that we should be able to do it alone. She was truly surprised that I fought back, as I was always such a good little mama's boy. And she let it go. I also remember being pissed off at Mark, assuming he'd told on me.

That night when we went to sleep (in the same bed, as usual), Mark and I didn't talk much. It felt gross. Like there was a distance. But I still felt I was right to want to do this business my own way, with my friend Brandt, without Mark.

The next morning when I woke up, I went into the backyard to check on the box. The first thing I noticed was that there was no box. There was, however, a pile of rusty nails and rather violently torn apart pieces of wood. As if the Tasmanian Devil himself had torn through our neighborhood to take great vengeance upon my box.

Our dad was at work and our mom was also out, and I remember seeing Mark sitting in the living room watching TV. But I could tell he was waiting for me to find the box. He didn't look at me. He waited for me to come to him. Now, I'm the older brother, but there is something just fucking intimidating sometimes about Mark. There's a deep darkness there. I share it. But to see it in a five-year-old kid who has just destroyed a (sort of) solid wooden box is a little daunting. But I didn't give a shit. I was feeling like Jeffrey Lebowski and Papa George Bush at this point: "This aggression will not stand." I turned off the TV and waited for Mark to look at me. It took him a little bit. He turned his head and stared at me. He said nothing.

JAY: You want to tell me what happened to my box?
MARK: What happened to your box?
JAY: You didn't see it?

(*Mark didn't answer at this point. Well played.*)

JAY: Someone took a hammer and destroyed it.

(*Long pause.*)

MARK: I'm sorry that happened.
JAY: Did you destroy my box with a hammer?
MARK: Nope.

(*Long pause.*)

JAY: Did you destroy my box with any other kind of tool?
MARK: Nope.

(*Long pause.*)

JAY: Did you have anything to do with my box ending up like it is now?

(*At this point Mark went silent. I nailed him. But I was also thinking, "How the fuck did he do that without a tool?"*)

JAY: I'm going to tell Mom and Dad and you're gonna be in huge trouble.
MARK: I don't care about that.

At this point Mark looked at me. And I could see he was fighting back the emotion. He was giving me the "fuck you" look but the tears were already rolling down his cheeks. And all the anger just drained right out of me. I felt horrible. I felt horrible that I'd hurt his feelings. And I think I also felt horrible that I was, essentially, trapped in some way. That I was inextricably linked to Mark in a way that was already limiting the types of friends I could have and the types of things I might want to do. And I knew in my spirit that there was something incredibly beautiful and also inherently unhealthy about our relationship. And a big part of me wanted to dig in my heels and say that "this has to be okay, for me to do things without you." But I was only nine years old. And I loved my little brother. And I didn't understand all the things I was feeling.

So I went outside, took the hammer, and destroyed the rest of the box while Mark watched me from inside. I walked the pieces to the trash can and tossed them in. I did it slowly so he could see me doing it all. And when I was done, I came back in and sat down next to Mark. We turned the TV back on and watched whatever movie was on.

Later that night, I didn't tell on him to our parents. I think that, even at those early ages, we already knew our relationship was beyond what our mom and dad could police or even understand. We were building that nonverbal language that we still use today. Laying the track for the familiar blend of big love and heartbreak that only the two of us are capable of wielding upon each other.

CHILDREN OF THE MOUNTAINS

THIS IS THE story of how I liked one of Jay's new movie ideas so much that I accidentally murdered it. Like Lennie did to that sweet little puppy. (FYI, I'm writing this alone because Jay would try to be nice to me and make me feel less terrible about what I did, but I'd rather just tell it like it happened.)

I was in Maine on vacation with Katie. Jay and I were coming off of a particularly long run of intense work together. During this time, we were both feeling the need for a little space. Also during this time, Jay came up with an interesting movie idea that didn't necessarily fit into our "brand" at the time. We were becoming known for making quirky dramedies, and we planned to make a few more that stuck to that mold before we ventured off into uncharted territory. But as we all know, you can't stop ideas from coming to you. And Jay had come up with a loose concept for a moody, dramatic movie he was calling *Children of the Mountains*. He didn't have much, but he knew it should involve a teenage girl from a small town who is estranged from her mother, plus this girl's not-so-nice boyfriend, her chubby male best friend, and their adventure together through the wilderness to find her mother.

Since I was on vacation and we were looking for a little

break anyway, Jay planned to work on the idea by himself for a bit. Jay and I would talk on the phone every day about something business-related, and I would ask him how the movie idea was coming along. The more he explained the world and feel to me, the more excited I got about what it could be. So I asked him to send me something on paper whenever he felt it was ready. Normally we share things with each other right away. It's almost inevitable that the other's ideas will improve the project and help push it forward.

But Jay was . . . I don't want to say resistant, because it wasn't that. He was just kind of slow getting me some pages to read. Which was an anomaly for him. But I was on vacation, so I didn't push. Still, I remained excited and felt the idea starting to swirl in my own head. It was taking off and forming a life of its own inside my brain, whether I liked it or not.

By the next week, I still hadn't gotten any pages from Jay. So I pressed him to send me something. He was still hesitant, feeling it wasn't ready yet to be shared, but I assured him I just wanted to get a look at it because I was so genuinely excited about the idea. Which was true! He reluctantly sent me what he had written. And this is when it all got weird.

When I read the pages I was disappointed. I felt that the plotting was thin. That there were so many opportunities for a classic, great story that Jay was missing out on. Which was insane to me because, of the two of us, Jay in particular has a penchant for using standard genre structure to make our movies move at a fast clip. But this was . . . slow. And kind of boring. And I was shocked. I knew Jay was a better writer than this and I couldn't believe that he wasn't seeing all the opportunities I was seeing. Up until this point, Jay and I had shared the exact same creative instincts and taste. We had never come across a situation where I wanted the movie to go one way and he was seeing it a different way.

At the time, though, I was so excited about "my version" of this movie building steam in my head that I could only see that version. And it truly was a "good" version of the movie. Well plotted, well-developed character dynamics, good twists— the works. So I just assumed that Jay would be excited that I had cracked the code for *Children of the Mountains* and could elevate his movie idea beyond what he had been able to write.

I called him and, as a respectful creative partner, first complimented him on what I thought he did well. Then I excitedly launched into what I thought the script could be. Changing character dynamics, upping the plot quotient, walking Jay through an entire version of the movie that I had accidentally developed in my head over the past couple of weeks. I pitched it well. It sounded amazing. And when I was done . . . crickets.

I know Jay well enough to know when he's bummed out. And I could hear it in the silence on the other end. Yet he too is a respectful creative partner. So he thanked me for my thoughts on the movie and said he needed a beat to let it all settle in his brain. And all I could think was "What's there to settle? I just cracked the code of an amazing movie! We could go make this thing!" But I didn't say anything. I hung up. Confused. And a little soul-sick. I couldn't figure out what went wrong.

My first thought was that I had damaged his ego. Maybe he couldn't stand the thought of his little brother being able to crack a better movie out of his idea than he had. But that didn't make sense. We never had that sense of ego with each other when it came to the work. Over and over again through the years, we've always had the philosophy of "best idea wins," and we were just as happy for either one of us to come up with that idea.

So I just sat in this gross feeling for a while. And when Jay and I talked the next day about more business stuff, neither of us talked about *Children of the Mountains*. It had somehow become the diseased elephant in the room, and eventually I couldn't stand it anymore. So I just jumped in. . . .

MARK: Hey. Can we talk about *Children of the Mountains*?

(Pause.)

JAY: Sure.
MARK: Good, cuz I'm feeling weird about it and I don't know what happened and I don't know what to do.
JAY: Yeah. It's . . . kinda hard. I'm still figuring it out.
MARK: Do you wanna . . . just . . . try to talk it out with me?
JAY: Um . . . okay.

(The breath. Fuck.)

JAY: So, you're an incredible writer. And that version of the movie you came up with is kinda undeniably . . . great.

(This is not what I was expecting to hear. I am momentarily relieved, but it might just be my ego feeling that. Not sure yet.)

JAY: And . . . I guess what's been hard for me is that I'm . . . I'm trying to do something a little different with this one?
MARK: Okay.

JAY: Like . . . I'm trying to give it the space to breathe and tell me what it wants to be. And admittedly that vibe is something maybe more atmospheric, poetic, odd, whatever . . . something that doesn't look as good on paper as what you are seeing for this movie.

(*A tough silence.*)

JAY: And the truth is I don't really know exactly what this movie wants to be. But I'm interested in slowly chasing it, instead of grabbing it and just . . . jamming it into the place that we already know exists for it. Because we've already done that thing. And I want to do this one differently.

(*This breaks my heart. I understand it now. And Jay feels my heartbreak and immediately jumps to my aid with some compliments to soften the blow.*)

JAY: And you are so good at making that movie into something that works. So quickly. But it also makes me doubt myself and what the movie can be. And it kinda puts a cloud over the movie, while I'm still in the phase of trying to get some light on it. I know that sounds corny, but . . .
MARK: No. I get it. You're, like, deep-sea fishing for a bigger, odder, newer way of telling a story. But I'm on the surface just catching fish after fish and it's hard to do what you're trying to do with all the noise up there.
JAY: Yeah. Kind of.

(*Silence. This sucks for both of us. He knows I meant well. I know he appreciates me. But it feels terrible. For both of us.*)

MARK: I'm so sorry. I think I just got excited and saw it. . . .

JAY: I know you did. And your version is awesome. And maybe better than anything I will eventually come up with. Which is part of what makes this so hard.

MARK: Okay.

(At this point I realize I need to back off and take his lead.)

MARK: So how should we proceed?

JAY: Um . . . I think I'm just gonna take some time with it. Let it marinate in my head . . . try to get back to that pulse I was chasing and see what comes.

MARK: That sounds good. Don't feel like you need to include me if you don't want to. But know that I'm here if you do wanna discuss it at any point.

JAY: Thanks. I really appreciate you being understanding. And I'm genuinely sorry that you feel like you have to apologize for being inspired and coming up with a brilliant version of my movie.

It ended here with both of us laughing. Jay is very good at giving this energy to our hard conversations. It's one of the things I love about him most. So we told each other we loved each other and hung up.

And we never talked about *Children of the Mountains* again. It was an unfortunate casualty of our intense collaboration. Jay couldn't find his way back in because of what I had done, and neither of us wanted to make the movie I came up with because of the way it had all gone down. And now we're both a little bit better at giving each other that critical time and space during the fragile mystery of birthing a creative idea.

ONE OUT OF FIVE

IT IS BEDTIME. You are wiped. Your kids are wiped. And your goals are at odds. You want them to go to sleep. They want to stay up. It's a perfect conflict, and one that in our experience does not resolve easily. In fact, we would argue that the great collaboration of parents as rule makers and children as rule followers is never more greatly tested than at bedtime. The essential conflict is simple: Most parents feel the need to lay down the law and make the law feel impenetrable. "This is our routine. We are sticking to it." And the children are normally smart enough to know that their only chance of "winning" (staying up past bedtime) is to disrupt that routine in any way possible. Basically a fucking nightmare.

Recently one of us had an experience with one of our daughters (we will leave out names to protect the innocent) that perfectly encapsulated this conflict. Daddy Duplass was trying to get Daughter Duplass into bed, and Daughter Duplass had a new balloon that she did not want to let go of. It went a bit like this:

DAD: Sweetheart, did you brush your teeth?
DAUGHTER: Yep.
DAD: Brush your hair?

DAUGHTER: Yep.

DAD: Okay. Thank you. Let's get you to bed, love.

DAUGHTER: Okay.

(Daughter dutifully heads for bedroom, still holding balloon.)

DAD: Let's leave the balloon out here, sweetie.

(Pause. Daughter is thinking. An idea comes.)

DAUGHTER: But I want to sleep with my balloon.

(Pause. Dad is now thinking. He knows that if he allows this little girl to bring the balloon into her room, there will be no sleeping tonight. There will only be playing with the balloon.)

DAD: I don't think that's a good idea.

DAUGHTER: Why not?

DAD: Because balloons are for playing, not for sleeping.

(The ridiculous shit we say as parents continues to surprise us.)

DAUGHTER: But I not going to play with it. I only going to sleep with it.

(And now Dad sees "the play." If she continues to argue, even if she loses the argument she still gets to stay up later because she bought all this "awake" time by arguing. Even

better, if she actually wins the argument, then she gets to stay up that much later playing with the balloon. She has somehow, at four years old, gotten herself into a win-win argument like a skilled corporate trial attorney. Cornered and exhausted, Dad now has no choice but to go into power play mode.)

DAD: I'm sorry, sweetheart. That's just the way it is.

(*Pause. Quivering bottom lip now from Daughter. Is it real? Fake? Is there a difference? Shit.*)

DAUGHTER: But, Daddy . . . I cannot sleep without my balloon.

(*Aha! Dad realizes he has found a crack in her logic and the solution has laid itself bare. He has a chance after all.*)

DAD: Honey, you definitely *can* sleep without that balloon.
DAUGHTER: I can't.
DAD: Yes you can.
DAUGHTER: But I can't, Daddy!
DAD: Sweetie, I know for a fact that you can sleep without that balloon.
DAUGHTER: How?

(*Dad, excited, goes in for the kill.*)

DAD: Because you just got this balloon today. And I have known you your entire life. And for your entire life you have gone to sleep every single night without that balloon.

(Bam. Nailed it. And now Daughter knows she has been caught. But surprisingly she does not give up. Dad watches her as her eyes seem to search the room and her own brain for another tactic. Some new approach to win this argument. Or at the very least extend the argument to win more precious time before bed. Then suddenly it hits her and she begins to speak, piecing together an argument that bears an intelligence way beyond her years.)

DAUGHTER: Yes, Daddy, I know that. But . . . you see . . . all the nights that I *did* sleep before this one . . . those were nights that I did *not* have my balloon. And now I *do* have my balloon, and I cannot sleep without it. Anymore. Ever.

(And Dad takes this blow to the chin hard. It's a fantastic argument. It's been executed with clarity and relative precision. Fuck. He knows he really should honor this hard mental work of hers. But at the same time, he cannot let that balloon into her room or else she will not sleep. She will stay up and play with that damn balloon all night, and tomorrow will be Armageddon for the entire family due to this one little girl's lack of sleep. Dad has a decision to make. It's a big one. He must consider not only this girl and himself but the entire family. And he is tired. And maybe not at his best right now. So . . .)

DAD: Honey, I'm not going to argue with you anymore. I'm taking the balloon, and it's time for you to go to bed. And that's final.

And, with that, Dad takes his daughter into her bedroom. She cries hard but eventually calms down as he reads her an extra book and lies with her until she falls asleep. And then Dad goes downstairs to finally get his free time. The kids are asleep. He can relax now.

But he can't relax. Because he knows he screwed up. Because his daughter made an impeccably smart argument in the face of authority, and he shut it down with the blind hammer of a brute squad. And while he realizes he had her "best interests" in mind (getting her some good sleep so she won't be exhausted the next day), he did not consider some longer-range interests of hers. That she is a girl. And that he is a man. And that one of the major lessons he needs to teach his daughter is that, with intelligence and a clear, strong, fair argument, she can topple any figure of authority that stands in the way of her goals. Particularly a male figure of authority.

Fuck.

So Dad beats himself up a little bit longer and then comes up with a plan. He calls it "One out of five." And he allows himself the luxury to maintain his authority over his daughter in four out of five arguments. This approach will generally keep order in the house. But on that fifth argument, that one that she truly earns a win on, he must concede that win to her. To empower her so that when she is twenty-two years old at her first job and looks up at that boss standing in her way, she has the innate confidence (and historical precedent) to know she can move through that boss and accomplish her goals.

And then Dad goes upstairs and puts the balloon in his daughter's room so that she can see it first thing when she wakes up. And watches her sleep for a bit longer. And he is flooded with equal parts lament and celebration that this child-parent collaboration is a complex puzzle whose grand mysteries will never fully reveal themselves.

TOP 10 FILMS OF ALL TIME (PART 6)*

American Movie

Raising Arizona

Tootsie

Rocky

Hoop Dreams

Dumb and Dumber

The Horse Boy

You Can Count on Me

Joe Versus the Volcano

Ordinary People

The final list. With two new movies we hadn't previously considered. Movies that not only were fantastic but truly rounded out our collective list, as their greatness was tied to viewing experiences we shared together. That time in Austin circa 1993 when we rented *Joe Versus the Volcano* because we realized one of our great modern playwrights, John Patrick Shanley, wrote and directed the film. And how pleasantly surprised we were to see that it wasn't a flop after all, but a highly intelligent, misunderstood adult fairy tale. Also—*Ordinary People.* The film we watched in the early 1980s (way too young) that taught us no matter how difficult things got between us, the thought of losing each other kept us eternally bound.

* The end.

XV.

When we made our second studio movie, *Jeff, Who Lives at Home*, the circumstances were perfect. Our friend Jason Reitman, who was the king of indie films that make lots of money, came on board to produce it and protect our way of filmmaking. Along with his financier, the wonderful Steve Rales, he curated the perfect environment for us. We made the exact film we wanted to make, we didn't have to battle anyone creatively, and it may be the thing we are most creatively proud of to this day.

But when the film came out, it didn't "hit" like we all wanted it to. It was well reviewed, and all the cinephiles came to see it, but it didn't cross over into the mainstream like we'd hoped it might. In the end, everyone barely broke even and we all walked away feeling disappointed that our little gem of a movie had not traveled further. What we didn't know at the time was that the middle class of independent film was beginning its decline. That's to say, all of those midsize independent films like *Juno* and *Little Miss Sunshine* that used to cross over and break out were now just limping across the finish line. People were watching their "indie" movies at home on Netflix or iTunes. And they were also starting to watch the various amazing television shows being offered by the renaissance in cable programming.

So what we ended up doing was focusing a bit on the smaller films that we knew how to make well. We produced tons of little movies like *Safety Not Guaranteed, Your Sister's Sister, The One I Love, The Overnight,* and *Tangerine,* among others. These were movies we could pay for ourselves, sell later at film festivals, and share our profits from with our cast and crew. It was all going well, but we didn't have that one singular project that we wanted to write and direct together that normally took up most of our year. As a result, I had extra time on my hands while Mark was carrying the bulk of the producing load and I was acting in projects outside of our brotherhood, like *Transparent.*

With this extra time, I started meeting with our good friend Steve Zissis and discussing a small TV show that would be made specifically for HBO GO's digital online platform. It was called *Alexander the Great,* and it was based on Steve and his life. It was a way to show the world what an immense talent we believed Steve to be.

When we brought the project to HBO, they decided they wanted it to be not only bigger but one of their premium Sunday night shows. They also wanted it to be about two couples instead of just one. At this point, Mark was brought more heavily into the process, and we found ourselves asking a big question about where we were headed with our careers. Were we willing to take on and run a TV show for HBO? We had mostly shied away from creating TV, as we'd heard what a time suck it could be and wanted to leave ourselves enough time to write and direct movies. But it seemed that, considering the decline of the kinds of movies we used to direct and the emergence of this new wave of great TV programming, the universe was ushering us toward this HBO show.

So we signed on to write and direct all eight episodes of the first season of what would become *Togetherness*. Mark would star alongside Steve, and we cast the incredible Melanie Lynskey as Mark's wife and Amanda Peet as Melanie's sister and Steve's eventual love interest. The goal was to create a simple show. A show that was specifically "low concept," if there is such a thing. A show just about people as we knew them, and their seemingly small but insurmountable interpersonal issues. What we didn't realize then was that it would be the most challenging time we've ever faced as brothers.

We used to joke that *Togetherness* was a show about trying to get as close as you could to the people you loved, and then once you achieved that high level of intimacy, realizing that you needed them to GIVE YOU SOME FUCKING SPACE! It was a funny, sweet conflict that we knew quite well. It turned out to be one that we faced as brothers, over and over again, on the actual making of *Togetherness*. From being together every day in the writers' room to our thirteen-hour days on set while shooting to being together in the edit room every day after that. And then, as soon as season one was done, realizing that we would be starting season two right away and facing that full brothers immersion all over again.

But HBO loved our show. Audiences seemed to love our show. And as much as we were getting a little beat up by the intense schedule, it seemed like we were doing good work and we should keep going. After all, it was every storyteller's dream to run a show on a channel like HBO.

But we were both feeling anxious heading into season two. About having to compromise on each other's work rhythm and pace. About the long hours and lack of personal space. About how having both of us in the same room over long periods of time is almost like trying to breathe the same supply of oxygen. And how there only seems to be enough for one of us. But every time we started to complain, we would laugh at ourselves. WE HAVE A FUCKING SHOW ON HBO! PEOPLE LIKE IT! WHAT ARE WE COMPLAINING ABOUT?

So we rushed headlong into season two, and it was even more difficult than the first. We were promoting season one while working on season two. Mark was still shooting *The League*. I was now acting on *Transparent*. We were producing an entire slate of movies for Netflix. We had signed on to write this book. We were . . . fucking bananas.

Needless to say, we started to shut down a little bit. Less socializing. Less exercising. More emotional eating. Everything was out of whack. We really only had time for work and our families. And the strangest thing happened: Even though we were spending more time together than we ever had, we started to become strangers. Our brotherhood and friendship started to get swallowed by all of the work we were sharing. In essence, we were becoming more business partners and less brothers.

Reviews of season two were great, our viewership was steady, and our network loved the show. So when HBO provisionally greenlit another season after we wrapped, we opened up the writers' room for season three. Everything was going our way. It felt like we were going to be making this show for a good six seasons or so. And that was all exciting, except for the fact that we were kinda miserable.

So we talked about it for a bit. We even made a list of the

pros and cons of our situation. And as we looked at that list (almost all pros, by the way) we immediately felt like whiny assholes. HBO was going to pay us to make the exact show we wanted to make. With our friends. In our neighborhood. And we had the audacity to complain about it in any way, shape, or form? We were grossed out by our own ingratitude and quickly resolved to put our heads down and launch into season three of *Togetherness* with positivity and a renewed sense of appreciation for our situation. There. Done. Moving on.

Less than a week later we got a call from HBO saying that we needed to close up our writers' room for season three. *Togetherness* was being canceled.

I AM JEALOUS

IT IS NOT easy to have a little brother who is so good at so many things. Particularly considering that, in the first fourteen years of our relationship, I was better at all things. But now I have a little brother who is a fully grown man, a man not only good at many things but better than me at many things. Frankly, this sucks.

By the time Mark was fifteen, he was playing guitar and writing songs that were beyond his years . . . and mine. At the time, I couldn't handle the thought that he might be more advanced or simply better at these things. So whenever he played me a song that he had written by himself, I would give him enough encouragement to make him feel good and keep going, but I also made sure to hold my semi-professorial position with him. Or rather, above him. The constructive criticism was partly designed to affirm that I was still the big brother and thus the authority on all things. I didn't even realize what I was doing at the time, and in hindsight I'm disgusted with myself for behaving this way.

I was threatened . . . terrified that I was turning out to be the Beau Bridges character in *The Fabulous Baker Boys* (the less talented older brother, desperately trying to retain some footing), or worse, the Fredo. The harder truth is that I still feel threatened. While we are writing this very book, Mark often disappears to bang out a few chapters at a blistering and incomprehensible pace. They are usually inspired and great, and I absolutely give him the props he deserves. But unfortunately I'm also a little jealous. Which, as mentioned before, sucks.

And the suckiness is a layered suckiness. Suckiness level one is fairly obvious: I don't want to feel less than my creative partner, particularly one who is younger and who used to be, essentially, my pupil. But the deeper level of suck is that I beat myself up for feeling this way. I constantly have to remind myself that we are part of a collaboration, that we are complementary, and any strengths he has also benefit me. Any resentment I feel regarding his talent and success is petty and needs to be transcended. But sometimes I just can't beat it, and I get down on myself for not being a better and bigger person.

This is when I turn to my journal. I write passage after passage about the challenge and beauty of our collaboration but also the courage I seek to be my own man and stand on my own merits. Journaling helps, but year after year the entries sound unnervingly repetitive. I realize I will always be struggling with this in some shape or form. It will ebb and flow randomly like the rivers and tides in the dorky nature documentary I watch to calm myself down. Perhaps feeling threatened and jealous is natural . . . maybe even okay? If so, I just hope Mark gets jealous of me too.

I AM ALSO JEALOUS

FOR YEARS, JAY and I would walk into a film festival or similar industry event and be greeted with big smiling faces. Because people love brother teams. They love that we work together, and they think we're interesting because of it. And we get off on this attention. Because we're human. And because we were so summarily ignored by the public for the first ten years of our creative partnership.

And then I got cast in a television show called *The League* and became a more recognizable face. And as we entered these same kinds of parties, people started to notice me first. And maybe talk to me a little bit more than Jay. It wasn't egregious, but it was real. We both felt it. And while I found this to be very unfair to Jay, I have to admit something gross: I also secretly liked it. And this was a disgusting feeling that I wanted nothing to do with. Was it not enough to be the indie filmmaker brother duo who is greeted with a smile? I also had to be the "more prominent" brother inside that very duo?

Ewwww. Fucking ewwww.

But it's the way I felt. I couldn't help myself. I liked the attention. I wanted to transcend that gross feeling, but I simply couldn't.

And as the years went by, Jay began to stay home from some

of these parties. Because it made him feel bad that many of the people just wanted to talk to the Duplass face that they recognized from television or our movies. It wasn't something Jay was morose about, it was just one of those things that we both understood as an "It is what it is" kind of thing.

And then Jay and I met with Mindy Kaling to discuss her acting in one of our movies. A week later, she actually called us and asked if we'd be willing to take recurring roles on her new show, *The Mindy Project,* as midwives who were also (wait for it) brothers. We were astonished and utterly flattered that she asked us. And we also found it odd that she wanted Jay to act, since he had no previous acting experience. It wasn't necessarily that Jay wasn't interested in acting. It was just that, from the first video camera our dad brought home, Jay had always held the camera and I had always been in front of the camera, so we legitimately never considered Jay as an actor before. But it seemed too fun to pass up. So we accepted, and over the next few years had a blast together playing these overly PC midwives on network television.

A few years later, Jay went to a party and met Jill Soloway, who asked for his advice on casting a brand-new "web show" she was making for Amazon. She needed a quirky, funny, mid-thirties Jewy dude who could play a bit of a jerk and still garner sympathy from the audience. Jay recommended every male actor he knew in that age range, and none were quite right for Jill. Then she simply looked at Jay and said, "It's you." And that is how Jay came to star in *Transparent.* And that is how Jay became an actor.

And that is when our experience showing up to industry parties started to shift. Because *The League* had now finished its run. I was working behind the scenes on a new show that would become *Togetherness,* and Jay ended up being the one on a television series for everyone to see. And Jay was now the brother that people wanted to talk to at the industry parties. Moreover, the kinds of conversations he was engaging in were like none I'd previously experienced while in his position. They were, to put it bluntly, of a much deeper, rewarding, and emotionally enriching nature because they were about the trans rights movement and the complex nature of family as opposed to the puerile (albeit hilarious) dick jokes of my former show *The League*.

And that odd, gross pride I took in being the brother everyone wanted to talk to was immediately replaced with jealousy. And I had a hard time transcending that feeling. And it made me feel doubly gross. Because I love my brother and am so happy for him to get the type of praise he has been robbed of and deserving of for so many years. And because inside of me, right next to my pride in him, is a little green monster throwing petty jealousy darts. And hitting targets pretty consistently.

And it makes me want to be a better brother.

XVI.

WE WEREN'T IN the same room when we got the call that *Togetherness* was being canceled. Our bosses explained that there was some internal restructuring going on and that *Togetherness* was unfortunately caught in the crossfire. We took the high road, thanked our bosses for two great seasons, and let them off the hook for feeling so terrible about blindsiding us. And when we hung up with them, we didn't call each other back (which we always do). I remember waiting for Jay to call. And thinking that he was probably waiting for me to call him. But neither of us did. At least not right away.

I was extremely upset at first. I was feeling all the wonderful things one feels when one gets fired. Rejection. A sense of failure. Embarrassment. Even a bit of the old "You don't realize how good you had it with us!" And that stuck for a while. But I didn't want to call Jay and put that on him. I didn't know what he was feeling, and I felt like I needed to give him some space to experience whatever he wanted to feel without me putting my feelings on top of his.

The next day we got in touch and scheduled a hike. We didn't speak for quite a while. . . .

MARK: So. How are you feeling about it all?

JAY: Um . . . still pretty confused.

MARK: Yeah. Me too.

JAY: It's like that George Carlin joke about someone burying an ax in your face. How it definitely hurts, but there's also that cool blast of air on your brain that's actually . . . actually quite nice.

(*Again. Jay always good with the jokes in these situations. I will always love this about him.*)

MARK: I feel it too.

JAY: You do? It's weird. It's like . . . would I have ever chosen to give up the incredible bird in hand that *Togetherness* was? No way. But . . .

MARK: But now that it's not an option . . .

(*Giggling. Devilish, secret giggling.*)

JAY: Kinda nice to think about all that extra time we'll have.

MARK: Maybe get life back in balance a little bit.

JAY: Take a walk? Exercise?

MARK: Play with the kids . . .

JAY: Or read a fucking book.

MARK: God. Yes. What are those things?

JAY: Yeah. I'm glad you're feeling it. I was worried I was gonna be alone in this one.

MARK: Nope. I'm right there.

(*It feels nice to agree. To be together on this idea. Because there is a bigger issue to be discussed. We both know it. And we both are terrified to bring it up.*)

JAY: Remember last time we took this trail we were talking about me directing a movie on my own . . .
MARK: . . . and I lost my shit.
JAY: Ha! You were fine.
MARK: Whatever. I was terrified. I . . . I wasn't ready to handle anything other than utter brotherly codependence.

(Jay smiles at me. It is at once funny, sweet, and sad. It occurs to me that I spend most of my time writing movies that can tee up a moment like this. Where people who love each other are about to break something new open. And are afraid it will change them forever.)

MARK: But I think that . . . I think that if you brought that same issue up to me today, I could handle it . . . better.
JAY: Yeah?
MARK: Yeah. I mean . . . look. You're my big brother. I'm always going to look up to you and want to be with you in many ways. But . . .

(Silence.)

JAY: But maybe it's okay if we get a little space?
MARK: Yeah. Maybe. I think that might be the cool blast of air on your brain you're feeling.
JAY: I think so too.

(We both start to cry. But it's a good one. It feels like a healthy one.)

MARK: I've been missing the way we used to be together. Summers in the nineties. Steely Dan . . .

JAY: Making shitty movies and covering Lionel Richie on acoustic guitars?

MARK: Yeah.

JAY: Yeah, I miss it too.

MARK: And I really don't know how to get that back. Or if we can.

JAY: Yeah, me neither. But . . . I'm glad we're talking about it.

MARK: Do you think . . . do you think that our working relationship has somehow hurt our relationship as brothers?

(We both consider this for a while, neither of us ready to answer that question. So we just hike the rest of the way in silence, which also feels nice.)

AIRPORT

#4

(We are seated at a JFK gate that is nowhere near our actual departure gate. But when we saw these two dudes coming through security we were fascinated by their dynamic. So we followed them. Two musicians who seemed to be in their mid-thirties, guitars slung over their shoulders, a tired gait, and a comfort with each other that most rock stars don't have. When they sat down, we realized they were actually much younger. Early to mid-twenties, maybe. But their eyes were dark and their faces beat up. Something we knew and felt deeply.)

JAY: Best friends.

MARK: Childhood best friends.

JAY: Uh-huh. Lived on the same street. Six houses down.

MARK: They made a plan for their eighth birthdays. One would get the drum set.

JAY: One would get the guitar.

MARK: But they would learn both.

JAY: Of course.

MARK: And they got pretty good.

JAY: Fast. They started a duo band. All covers. They were called . . .

(We think on this for a moment. Gotta get it right.)

MARK: Doomsday?
JAY: Flashback?

(Giggling. Good ones. But not great yet.)

MARK: Vitality?
JAY: Blatant Vitality!
MARK: Yes!
JAY: Ha! It makes no sense!
MARK: Exactly! That's why it's perfect!

(We look at the two boys across from us. They are so tired. And their skinny jeans and T-shirts seem stretched out, worn for at least a few days without washing.)

JAY: They wrote their first original song about the girl who almost came between them.
MARK: Ooh. Good.
JAY: And they played it at her friend's party on dual acoustic guitars.
MARK: They did not change her name.
JAY: And they turned from dorks into music legends in their high school.
MARK: Best friends.
JAY: Best friends.

(We look back at the boys now. They are each pulling at their beards in the same manner. And both of their right legs are crossed over their left. And then we look back at each other and panic. Because we know instantly that these are not

best friends. These are brothers. Mark accidentally lets it
slip. . . .)

MARK: Fuck.

(But I am feeling it too. As if we subconsciously set a trap for
ourselves by following these two brothers. A trap that would
force us into a pit that we would have to fight our way out of.
Our fun little game was turning into something else. We both
felt it. We didn't really want to play it anymore but kinda
knew we had to.)

MARK: My guess is they have been on tour.
JAY: Yeah. They're flying home from a long tour.
MARK: Probably not a glamorous one, judging from the state
of their eye sockets.
JAY: Nope. Van tour. Splitting $142 a night. Sleeping on floors.
MARK: Trying desperately to hang on to that dream of becoming rock stars. The one they built when they were eight years
old.
JAY: Scared shitless that it won't come true. Knowing they are
probably pot committed at this point. No real turning back
once you've skipped college and gone headlong into your
dream.

(A beat. That was easy enough to do. An objective analysis.)

MARK: Yeah, they know they're in it for good. But . . . there's
another question lingering. One of them has been thinking
about . . . well . . .

(Are we doing this?)

JAY: The solo project?

MARK: Yeah.

JAY: It happens. There's nothing wrong with thinking about it. It's natural.

MARK: Absolutely. You work so hard and closely with someone for so long, you inevitably wonder what you can do on your own.

JAY: Will it be more fun?

MARK: Maybe. Will the stuff you make be as good without your partner?

JAY: Scary to think about it. On a bunch of levels.

MARK: Right? Am I just riding the coattails of the more talented one?

JAY: Am I carrying dead weight and is this partnership holding me back?

MARK: Will people even accept me if I'm only half of the partnership they've come to know and judge me by?

(We watch the boys. And they actually catch us looking at them. And they smile the same sad smile that we smile for people who have enjoyed watching us over the years. It's an incredibly profound moment somehow.)

JAY: The funny thing is, as they think about all of this stuff—all these confusing elements in their creative partnership— they've forgotten one thing.

(Mark looks at me. He genuinely has no idea what I'm going to say.)

JAY: Their friendship.

*(Mark looks away. He doesn't want me to see his face. Like
the hikes. We will look forward from this point on.)*

JAY: How the management of all these creative and business
partnership dynamics have taken their toll on that pure element of friendship that brought them together in the first place.
MARK: Like when the older one would come home from college and they would just hole up together for twenty-four
hours, playing music, hanging out, watching movies. Not so
much about making art and bringing it to the world but
just . . . being together.
JAY: Or even further back. When they would go to that shitty
waterslide park off Veterans Highway and just . . . ride water-
slides all day.
MARK: You mean the happiest years of their lives?
JAY: *(laughing)* Yep.

(We both laugh for a while. A hard laugh. There's a lot in it.)

MARK: Yeah. They both really want to have that conversation.
JAY: But they're terrified.
MARK: It'll probably happen in the least likely of places.
JAY: Like in parking lot 3F at the airport after they land.
MARK: With a loud-ass dump truck in the background inter-
rupting them.

*(We laugh some more, knowing that life's pivotal moments
always happen in these oddly mundane places.)*

JAY: And one of them will just . . . start spilling it.
MARK: Yep.

(Pause. A long one. And as usual when things get hard, we both remember that no matter what, I am still the older brother and I am ultimately willing to run into the burning building first when it really counts.)

JAY: About how sad they are that they can't be everything they want to be for each other.

MARK: That the friendship has changed.

JAY: That they have changed as people.

MARK: And that there's very little they can do to control it.

JAY: And that the creative partnership will take many different permutations through the years.

MARK: Some easy, some really fucking hard.

JAY: And it'll all feel so confusing and sad. And full of potential love and lost love.

MARK: A deep, unknowable history that they are fully submerged in.

(We look up and realize that the two brothers across from us are now gone. And it's about time for us to head to our gate. But we don't move. We both know we're not finished. That we don't want this story to end just yet. Or like this.)

JAY: And then . . . one of them asks the other one to get into his car. He wants him to hear something.

(Mark thinks on this a bit. I feel that he is uncertain where I am headed. And then, the rest of the story "flops" out before him. And he looks at me. And I can see in his eyes that he hopes like hell his flop is the same as my flop right now. That we can be the same again for this moment.)

MARK: It's a new demo.

JAY: (*smiling*) Yep.

MARK: Something he wrote on his own.

JAY: He's terrified to show it to his brother.

MARK: But he desperately needs him to hear it. Because if he can't share these things with him . . .

JAY: It's like they didn't happen. So he plays the song.

MARK: They sit in silence.

JAY: And the song is really good. And the fact that the song is this good is actually a great and terrible thing.

MARK: It means they can make art on their own. That they don't necessarily *need* each other to make something that's good. Which is great.

JAY: And terrible. But . . . the brother who just heard the song for the first time says to the other one, "It's weird. It almost feels like . . . like I wrote that song too. I can feel myself in it."

(*This thought changes the air around us. Somehow lifts both of our shoulders. Mark in particular takes great comfort and strength in it.*)

MARK: Right. As if all the time, energy, and love that they have shared have created a truly inextricable link between them. That no matter what happens, they will always exist inside of each other. And for one to make something truly on his own is . . . kind of . . .

JAY: Impossible. Because once you've joined souls with someone it's forever.

(*We sit in this for a bit. Because it's the greatest place to be. And we want to hang on to it for as long as it will last.*)

THE WATERSLIDE

So BACK IN Metairie in the early eighties there was a low-rent waterslide park off Veterans Highway. It only had a few slides, but one of them was (in our eyes) enormous. You had to be at least forty-eight inches tall to ride it. I was maybe forty-four inches. On a good day. So when we reached the top of the stairs, Jay would engage the lifeguard in polite conversation as she tried to make sure I was of proper height. I placed my waterslide mat down in front of my feet to hide the fact that I was on my tippiest of toes. As Jay continued to noisily babble into the lifeguard's ear, I fixed her with my best "Fuck you, you don't scare me" face as my tiny head barely crested the forty-eight-inch mark.

"You're good."

And with that, Jay jumped onto the slide first and took off. He rounded the corner, out of sight, and the lifeguard gave me the cue to go ahead. What she didn't know was that Jay had not only abandoned his safety mat, he was suspended just around the bend, arms planted firmly on the walls of the tube as the water rushed violently past him, waiting for me to come barreling down toward him.

The plan was simple: Before I crashed into Jay, I would jettison my own safety mat and lock arms and legs with him, effectively creating a Duplass Transformer. This new beast (now doubled in weight and sans safety mats) shot down the waterslide at a speed with which the insurance companies would not have been pleased. Without the mats, the small crevices where the tubes connected would scratch and scrape our backs, but we didn't care. We had serious speed. Even the extra sunblock oil on our arms and legs gave us (at least in our minds) a few extra mph.

We flipped over each other, arms and legs intertwined, hurtling toward the pool below, where most of the time there was another lifeguard waiting for us (holding our forsaken mats, warning us that what we had done was not only against the rules but also dangerous). One more infraction and we would be kicked out of the park for good. But we didn't care. We made our own rules. This was our way.

We climbed the stairs and went down the slide again.

FRIENDS OF THIS BOOK

THANK YOU TO Pamela Cannon and the fantastic staff at Ballantine Books, without whom this book would be intensely less readable. Actually, it wouldn't be readable at all. Or even here.

To Lauren Budd, who at nineteen years old was able to crack the difficult code of how to grammatically voice a personal book authored by two people. And to Lauren's also-brilliant mother, Mary Budd, for writing down on a yellow sticky pad, during breakfast, three title suggestions, one of which became the title of this book.

To Sloan Harris, Kristyn Keene, Joanne Wiles, Sydney Fleischmann, Carolyn Craddock, Duncan Birmingham, Alex Lehmann, and Nick Kroll for reading, then feeding back/reading, then feeding back/reading, then feeding back . . .

And to Katie, Jen, Ora, Molly, Mimi, Sam, Duckie, and Pups for loving us and letting us give our love to them even though we are not always great at it.

ABOUT THE AUTHORS

MARK DUPLASS and JAY DUPLASS are the critically acclaimed filmmakers behind *The Puffy Chair*, *Baghead*, *The Do-Deca-Pentathlon*, *Cyrus*, and *Jeff, Who Lives at Home*. For HBO, they wrote and directed *Togetherness*, produced the animated series *Animals*, and created the anthology series *Room 104*. Their producer credits also include the feature films *Safety Not Guaranteed*, *The Skeleton Twins*, and *Tangerine*. As an actor, Mark has appeared on the hit comedy *The League* and in such films as *Your Sister's Sister*, *The One I Love*, and *Blue Jay*, while Jay has a leading role on the Golden Globe–winning series *Transparent* and has appeared in such films as *Landline*, *Beatriz at Dinner*, and *Outside In*. Both brothers had recurring roles on *The Mindy Project*.

Twitter: @jayduplass
Twitter: @MarkDuplass

ABOUT THE TYPE

The text of this book was set in Filosofia, a typeface designed in 1996 by Zuzana Licko, who created it for digital typesetting as an interpretation of the eighteenth-century typeface Bodoni, designed by Giambattista Bodoni (1740–1813). Filosofia, an example of Licko's unusual font designs, has classical proportions with a strong vertical feeling, softened by rounded droplike serifs. She has designed many typefaces and is the co-founder of *Emigre* magazine, where many of them first appeared. Born in Bratislava, Czechoslovakia, in 1961, Licko came to the United States in 1968. She studied graphic communications at the University of California, Berkeley, graduating in 1984.